PENGUIN BOOK

Five foot and FEARLESS

Photo by S. Burridge

Liz Williams joined the Air Force as a teenager before embarking on a career in the New Zealand Police. She has served in both the Criminal Investigation Branch and the General Duties Branch, as well as having a role in the Armed Offenders Squad. Liz now lives in Central Otago with her husband, son and a host of slightly irritating animals that no one else wanted. She still works for the New Zealand Police.

LIZ WILLIAMS

Five foot and FEARLESS

A woman on the front line
in New Zealand's
Armed Offenders Squad

PENGUIN BOOKS

Note: To preserve the anonymity of the author's fellow AOS squad members, their names have been replaced with initials.

PENGUIN BOOKS
Published by the Penguin Group
Penguin Group (NZ), 67 Apollo Drive, Rosedale,
Auckland 0632, New Zealand (a division of Pearson New Zealand Ltd)
Penguin Group (USA) Inc., 375 Hudson Street,
New York, New York 10014, USA
Penguin Group (Canada), 90 Eglinton Avenue East, Suite 700, Toronto,
Ontario, M4P 2Y3, Canada (a division of Pearson Penguin Canada Inc.)
Penguin Books Ltd, 80 Strand, London, WC2R 0RL, England
Penguin Ireland, 25 St Stephen's Green,
Dublin 2, Ireland (a division of Penguin Books Ltd)
Penguin Group (Australia), 250 Camberwell Road, Camberwell,
Victoria 3124, Australia (a division of Pearson Australia Group Pty Ltd)
Penguin Books India Pvt Ltd, 11, Community Centre,
Panchsheel Park, New Delhi – 110 017, India
Penguin Books (South Africa) (Pty) Ltd, 24 Sturdee Avenue,
Rosebank, Johannesburg 2196, South Africa

Penguin Books Ltd, Registered Offices: 80 Strand, London, WC2R 0RL, England

First published by Penguin Group (NZ), 2012
1 3 5 7 9 10 8 6 4 2

Copyright © Liz Williams, 2012

The right of Liz Williams to be identified as the author of this work in terms of section 96 of the Copyright Act 1994 is hereby asserted.

Designed and typeset by Anna Egan-Reid, © Penguin Group (NZ)
Cover photograph by Rowan Williams
Cover art from iStockphoto.com
Printed in Australia by McPherson's Printing Group

All rights reserved. Without limiting the rights under copyright reserved above, no part of this publication may be reproduced, stored in or introduced into a retrieval system, or transmitted, in any form or by any means (electronic, mechanical, photocopying, recording or otherwise), without the prior written permission of both the copyright owner and the above publisher of this book.

ISBN 978 0 14 356693 9

A catalogue record for this book is available
from the National Library of New Zealand.

www.penguin.co.nz

Contents

1	Under the cover of darkness	7
2	Decisions, decisions	17
3	Pre-selection training	25
4	Lonely days and sleepless nights	33
5	National Selection	53
6	AOS qualifying course	87
7	The longest night	103
8	Operational	113
9	Angry men in wee villages	121
10	Moving on	127
11	Coming out of the closet	135
12	How to stop a car	143
13	Axeman	147
14	*Duccah, duccah, duccah*	155
15	Cowboys and baddies	163
16	Stop the car, I forgot the gun	169
17	Young lives cut short	175
18	Drugs, druggies and rugby tackles	181
19	Mixing it up in the farming community	185
20	Operation Pee	189

21	Criminals with jobs	199
22	Palmerston North's most wanted	205
23	One foot forward	213
24	The fame game	219
25	The Napier siege 2009	227
26	The last chapter	247
	Glossary	249

1
UNDER THE COVER OF DARKNESS

As I crept across the road in the team of five, my pulse racing, I wondered how in hell I was not going to be seen. The street lights up ahead were casting an eerie glow for 10 metres around their bases, and as I passed directly under each one, I was lit up for what felt like all the world to see. Well, for at least all of the population of the little village I was skulking through to see.

The black I was dressed in from head to toe silhouetted me beautifully against the lamps' light. A giant-sized shadow-puppet, fully armed with guns, grenades and Kevlar helmet. I tilted my head forward to check I wasn't about to fall over something on the ground in front of me, gripping my firearm tightly in my hands in anticipation of the stumble. My head-tilt just made my helmet, which I didn't seem to be able to get tight enough, slip forward and cover my eyes. A giant, armed – and now blind – shadow-puppet. Awesome.

I reached up with a gloved hand and shoved the headgear back, and also wiped off the large droplet of dribble that was hanging off the end of my nose. A head-cold has a time and a place; this was neither. After two more fruitless swipes, with more drops appearing as fast as they were wiped away, I gave up and just pulled my balaclava over my nose. All that could now be seen of my face was a set of worried-looking eyes and perhaps a darkened, soggy black mass of fabric over my still-dripping nose.

We continued moving along the fences toward the target address, counting mailboxes as we went. There was a gentle clicking sound as we progressed, of firearms and door-entry equipment hitting against other pieces of carried equipment. The sound was comforting – it let you know that even if you couldn't see the rest of the team behind you, they were still there.

Finally, looming in front of me was *the house*. It was set back from the road on a rise, had no lights on and, in the darkness, looked rather imposing. Stopping short, we hunkered down behind the neighbour's fence while one of the team crept forward to get eyes on the address. The rest of us huddled together, sorting out our plan of attack.

The whole front of the property was open to the street, so to get across to an area of cover on the other side, where we needed to be, would mean exposure for the required 20-metre dash. Getting to the sides of the house would be okay, as there were neighbouring properties which could be accessed. The rear was tricky due to high walls at the back, but another team had already set off around the other side of the block to cover there. After figuring out who was to go where, the team leader gave me my area of responsibility. 'You get across the open area and get as close as you can to the front of the house.'

Shit, shit, shit! This wasn't training any more – this was for real. What if I stuffed up one of the first jobs where I had a real position of responsibility? What if I compromised the whole team by getting spotted running across the front of the address? What if I *fell over*? But I didn't get time to consider all the 'what ifs' and 'yeah buts'. With my partner, Q, covering me, I scuttled across the open ground first, coming to a grateful, undiscovered halt behind a shed.

Poking my head out around the side of it, I checked the address.

No movement, lights or sounds in the five seconds I had taken to cross. Turning to where I'd come from, I beckoned for Q to come to me. Not taking my eyes off the front door, I kept watching for signs of life, soon hearing the sounds of Q's equipment gently rattling as he ran to my location. Scoping the garden area around us, we both selected our spot, then stealthily (or what I hoped was stealthily) moved to it, called in our positions over the radio, and settled in to wait.

I took stock of my situation. Although the walk in had only been two blocks, it had been hard work. I was still sweating and puffing from the effort. Wearing and carrying 20-something kilos of equipment on my 55-kilo frame meant that I felt every step we took. Being a member of the AOS (Armed Offenders Squad) wasn't the sort of job where you called a halt to the run so you could get your breath back. You just had to keep up. However, as I told myself – *You wanted to do this. Cope.*

Despite the physical tiredness, I was hyped with adrenaline and excitement. I was getting paid to do something many people would pay to do. I know it's not every sane person's cup of tea, but right there, at that moment, was exactly where I wanted to be.

As I lay in the darkness with silence all around me, I had a closer look at the spot I'd chosen to lay up in. In front of me was a hedge. It had a hole, which would afford a better view to the house and which I could try to wriggle through, but with all the equipment I was wearing it would be a risky manoeuvre and would also be quite noisy. But . . . being on the other side of the hedge would mean I would have a clear line of sight to the doorway where our offenders were likely to come out. I could also see a car parked close to the other side of the hedge that would give me good cover if I managed to get through. I thought to myself that if I got a chance, I would give it a try.

Waiting for a break in the radio traffic, I was just about to tell Q of my intentions when the silence was shattered by the local fire siren going off. In the still, clear night, it was terribly loud and sounded very close. I stared at the hole in the hedge and figured that the sound the siren made would cover the noise I'd probably make in getting through it. I wiggled a bit closer. In my earpiece I could hear the other team getting into position behind the property, but with still no break in the radio traffic, I had to make a decision. If the siren went up again, I would try to get through the hedge. There wasn't going to be time to confer.

'Whhhoooooooo . . .' Away it went in the upward blast of its wail. I threw myself at the hole and wriggled frantically. But my .223 firearm, which is roughly a metre long (and also known as an M4 or Bushmaster), immediately got snagged. I had one arm, my head and my shoulders through, but all my weapons – including my secondary weapon, the Glock pistol attached to my thigh – were now on the other side of the hedge. I couldn't even reach the PTT (press to talk) button on my radio to let Q know where I now was.

As the siren's wail went down I stopped moving and held my breath, then heard Q on the radio. He tried to call me but, with the button infuriatingly out of reach, I couldn't answer. I wriggled again to try to get my body through, after waiting for another siren blast to cover my noise. When Q got no reply, I heard him say to the AOS control base Zero Alpha, 'I don't know where she is – she's moved!' He sounded pretty brassed off. Bloody newbies.

My head now close to the back wheel of the car, the siren took off again, but then I heard what I thought were footsteps on gravel – probably the worst sound imaginable in my predicament. I had to remain silent as I could hear them approaching me. The next sound was what was quite possibly a set of car keys jiggling, and I began hoping like anything that the person I was hearing didn't get into the car.

Whoever it was, I couldn't challenge them as I wasn't free of the stupid bloody hedge; and I couldn't let anyone know where I was because of not being able to reach the bloody talk button. To make a bad situation even worse, I still couldn't see who belonged to the keys and the crunching feet as my bloody helmet had got pushed down over my eyes again.

I lay as close to the ground as my cumbersome outfit would allow and tried to look under the car to see who was making the noise and where they were. Such was the layering I was wearing that I rocked and rolled, like a Weeble wobbling (if you're too young to remember one of these, it's a little round toy that swayed from side to side but never fell down). And still I couldn't see anything.

As the siren went up yet again, I risked all by frantically wriggling, hoping that if the key-holder heard anything they would think I was a hedgehog, albeit a giant one. This time I managed to get my firearm through the hole, but I was still stuck. Like Winnie the Pooh in Rabbit's burrow. Then I heard a phone ring in the house.

The ring was accompanied by a pause in the crunching, then the sound of possibly – hopefully – retreating feet heading toward the sound of the ringing. With the next siren wail, I made a last concerted effort and burst through the hole. As I leapt to my feet and quickly snuck around the car toward where I'd heard the crunching gravel, I heard Q and another member of the team, G, yelling out a challenge. They must have seen what I had heard. 'Armed police! Put your hands in the air!' I joined them, closing in with firearm raised, my heart pounding; and inwardly cursing and muttering at my actions in getting snagged.

When I'd been through my training for the AOS, I remember clearly being told, 'No matter how tough your offenders are, when you have a loaded firearm pointed at them, they'll do anything you ask them to do.'

'Get your hands in the air! Get your hands in the air!' Q, now a lone voice so as to ensure the instructions were completely clear, continued screaming at our offender. Did he comply? Like hell he did. He defiantly thrust one hand in his pocket and began to pull something tiny out of it. He carried out this action with a flourish and with a clear intention to be belligerent and taunt us. His actions caused a flurry of challenging yells from Q, all of us poised with fingers hovering over the safety levers of our M4s. What had he pulled out of his pocket? Was it a gun?

As the offender had moved, he'd yelled out at the squad members challenging him to 'Bugger off!', his defiant words drowned out by Q's continued challenges. It was clear he hadn't read the manual on what to do when challenged with loaded firearms. This guy was everything I hadn't expected.

In a matter of only a few seconds, every squad member facing this target was making a multitude of decisions. What was in his hand? What options did we have? Did his actions amount to a threat to life? How long could we leave the decision to shoot or not to shoot? If we shot, what would be the bullet trajectory? Where were the other threats? What had our initial intell told us about him?

Many people rationalise about when they would or wouldn't shoot someone, but few appreciate the lack of time you have when faced with this ultimate choice. Everything happens in the blink of an eye. The official assessment of your split-second decision to take the shot takes weeks, months, or more probably years, and the ramifications of what you do, or don't do, will always be with you. But you don't exactly think ahead to a PCA (Police Complaints Authority) situation when choosing the best course of action. Instead, you concentrate on quickly making the best decision for the situation. Perhaps, at the back of your mind, is also the old saying: 'I would rather be judged by twelve, than carried by six.'

Always, whatever the situation, the decision to shoot or not shoot is yours, and yours alone. Not the media's. Not the public's. Not your boss's. Not your friends'. Yours. Your decision is always supported by law, but that doesn't make the frantic jumble of all the facts at that moment any easier to decipher.

With all these assessments rattling around in our heads, as quickly as the threat had appeared it disappeared again when the item in the man's hand was glimpsed. It was an asthma inhaler. It would have been a very small firearm, but the way he had presented it was more like a foolish attempt to commit suicide rather than just being belligerent when faced with the challenges we were issuing. In fact, it was just about the stupidest, potentially fatal thing anyone could ever do in such tense circumstances.

After further instructions were yelled, the man finally did what was asked and began walking forward to a safe area, muttering to himself, the inhaler now returned to his pocket. He was led out of my line of vision while I kept my eyes focused on the front-door area he had emerged from. Our earlier briefing suggested there was still someone inside.

Within seconds of Inhaler Man leaving my line of sight, a second male suddenly appeared at the doorway. I was momentarily distracted, however, by his outfit. He was decked out in a singlet worn under a brushed-cotton shirt, open at the front. On his lower half he wore a truly enormous pair of white Y-front undies, and sticking out of the bottom of this oversized, flapping mass of cotton was a set of the skinniest, whitest legs I had ever seen.

'Armed police! Get your hands up in the air! Get your hands in the air!' I immediately started screaming at him as he walked toward me. My loaded M4 was aimed squarely at his chest.

'Oh just calm down, calm down,' he scolded me. *Calm down?* What planet did these two come from?

Keeping his hands firmly wherever the hell he wanted, he stopped and looked around him. By now Q had returned, and while we yelled at this guy to comply *now*, Y-fronts took over from where his belligerent mate had left off and lectured us for being 'over the top'.

We needed to get him under control quickly, so – as he continued to berate us for being dramatic – I fumbled in the pockets of the utility over-vest that I wore outside my ballistic vest until I found what I was looking for: my canister of OC (pepper spray). I challenged the man and told him exactly what I would do if he didn't comply, and then proceeded to empty the can in his face when he didn't.

As I sprayed he turned his head away, and I effectively filled up his left ear. Not surprisingly, this had absolutely no effect on his level of compliance. Seeing that we were faced with someone who would continue to passively resist until the cows came home, another option was called for.

The rest of the team's M4s had lanyards attaching them to their over-vests, which meant that they could drop their firearms and these would stay connected, leaving them hands-free. But as I was the new person on the squad, my equipment wasn't yet all set up as it needed to be – the vest was inherited from a retired member, and it didn't have a lanyard. Placing my firearm on the ground so that I could grapple with an offender wasn't an option. I yelled at Q that I couldn't go hands-free – which he must have figured out from the fact I hadn't yet done anything. By the time the last words had left my mouth, he had grabbed Y-fronts and pulled him to the ground while I covered with my firearm.

Once Y-fronts was handcuffed, he was led away to where his offsider had been taken. Both were asked if there was anyone else in the house, and both answered no.

Our next job entailed clearing the house, to ensure that they were telling the truth. Surprisingly, they were. During the search of a bedroom, we found what had started the incident off – a firearm hidden in a cupboard. Prior to us getting called out, the house's occupant – the one now sitting outside in his giant undies – had popped next door and presented this firearm at his neighbours, because they were pissing him off. The neighbours had called the police. Both our offenders were drunk and clearly were not thinking rationally. That, hopefully, explained their stupidity when faced with our pretty clear instructions.

After clearing the house, Q and I holed up in their bathroom and splashed gallons of water on our faces. Since I had used my spray, we were both experiencing the residual effects of over-spray. That same stuff that had had no effect on Mr Y-fronts was irritating the hell out of both of us.

After the incident, we travelled back to our base, de-kitted, and debriefed. And less than an hour after that, I was back in my nice warm bed, finishing off an interrupted slumber. When I woke up next morning, it took me some time to figure out that what had happened had been reality – and not a very bad dream about a man who wore very bad underwear.

2

DECISIONS, DECISIONS

I don't think I can actually remember a time in policing when I didn't want to join the Armed Offenders Squad. My early reasons for joining probably weren't the purest, though – I just thought they looked really cool. I had joined the New Zealand Police in 1994 and, wanting to be part of this élite AOS, every few months from 1998 I put in a police report form expressing my eagerness. I always received the same reply: 'Thank you for your expression of interest. At this time there are no positions available.'

As time went by, I saw people around me join. They were boys. Big boys. Very capable boys, too. I became aware that perhaps my early reason for wanting to join – the coolness factor – was too transparent.

Some time into this continual application process, I was asked by a PNT (Police Negotiating Team) member if I wanted to join them. They went out with the AOS on call-outs, and their role was basically to negotiate a surrender; if the person refused, their house was stormed by the AOS. I thought that by accepting I would be close to where I wanted to go, so I took up the role with enthusiasm – still continuing with my AOS applications, however.

For four years, I wore a pager and went along to every call-out. The work was unpredictable and enjoyable; and, more often than not, in the middle of the night. I'd got married toward the end of the four years, but luckily, my husband was also in the Police and was used to broken nights. Then, one day in 2001 I was called in to a boss's office; I was told it was about my AOS applications. I held my breath. The news wasn't what I wanted to hear, though. I was a detective in the CIB (Criminal Investigation Branch) at the time, and I was told that because there were already a lot of serving AOS members in the CIB, the AOS was no longer recruiting from there. The reason for this rule was that when a serious crime occurred a CIB detective was often called out of the district, and worked through until the given job was completed. If the detective was also in the AOS, this affected their availability for AOS deployment.

I was crushed, to say the least. But it gave me a new direction. As long as I was in the CIB – a job that I enjoyed and wasn't about to leave – I wasn't ever going to be able to join the AOS. So instead, I decided to have a baby.

Now, don't get me wrong – getting knocked up wasn't a knee-jerk reaction to my rejection. I had completed a lot of career training already, and knew that if I was going to have children, this would be a good time for it. There was, and still is, a lot of support for cops – both men and women – taking time out to have a family, and whether I decided to return to work afterward or leave, I knew I would be well supported.

Time went by. I had my baby and was a very contented mother, housewife, baker of very bad biscuits, avid fan of daytime TV and part-time artist – of the starving variety. The artistic side of things was something I had been doing on and off since I was young, and in my last years of high school I had briefly toyed with the idea of going to art school. However, practicality won; the prospect of having no money to live on while painting nude people, mountains and pot plants lost out to a guaranteed income through full-time paid employment – hence I am Liz the police officer, not Liz the artist. Through motherhood I finally was able to return to art, if only momentarily.

I wasn't sure why I hadn't thought of doing this motherhood business years before. Someone should have told me that if you wanted a break from paid working for a living (note the paid bit), you should become a mother. I loved it. But all good things must come to an end, and as the coffers drained and my baby grew, I knew it was time to rejoin the ranks. So, in 2003 when my little one was aged nearly one, I decided to return to policing on a part-time basis.

To begin with, returning to work sucked rather a lot. Motherhood (and, I imagine, fatherhood) is made up of one part tolerance and nine parts of a very healthy dose of guilt. When I first went back, my lovely mother-in-law took on care duties for a few hours each day, but on returning home and seeing her run ragged by an exuberant toddler, I knew we had to find an alternative. Test two was day-care. I suffered the guilt of seeing that little face pressed up against the window as I abandoned him to go and fight crime. I suffered the guilt of feeling that I was letting work down when I sprinted out the door at one minute past my shift's end-time, or had yet another sick day when my son was struck down by yet another of the two million bugs that ran rife through the day-care facility. Why, oh why, had I not pursued the art thing?

But then things began to get a lot better. My son and I both adjusted – him much more quickly than me, as kids are apt to do. Before I knew it, a couple of years had ticked by where I enjoyed a balance of work and home life; then, in 2005, the AOS snuck its way back into my life. My husband was asked if he wanted to apply for the AOS as a sergeant. At the time, he was working as a section sergeant in Palmerston North. The AOS were predicting losing some squad supervisors, so he was asked to apply under that basis. I looked at him in disbelief. What a lucky bugger! All those reports I had written, all those aspirations I had harboured for all those years, and *he* got *asked!*

We talked about the ramifications of him being on the squad and me effectively staying as main 'caregiver' – what it would mean to family life. From my previous days of being a negotiator, I had a good knowledge of what squad work could entail in terms of call-outs, and neither of us thought that side of it would make a huge impact on our lives. Most friends and other people we spoke to who had one member of their family on a specialist squad in the police generally also had one parent outside the police, so their lifestyle changes were always going to be different from what ours might be. Neither of us was concerned about personal safety, both knowing that day-to-day front-line policing holds far more risks. When the AOS is involved, squad members are generally forewarned about the situation they are going into. Front-line police officers, on the other hand, face risk every time they make public contact – whether it's a routine car-stop or a door-knock. Those are the times an officer is likely to be hurt.

Having carefully weighed up all the options and considerations, we decided it was a goer. Putting my jealousy of what he was about to embark on to one side, I supported him in his efforts (in that I didn't hide his running shoes when he wanted to train). He subsequently completed two selection courses – one at district level and one national – then did a three-week qualifying course at Police College. Then he was away. An AOS member.

My life was again governed by a pager – this time my husband's, not mine. I lived vicariously through his call-outs, jealous as hell that it was him and not me. When he rolled back into bed at 3 a.m. after a call-out, I'd want to know where he'd gone, what he'd done, greedily absorbing all the details like I was starving.

I was, however, now fully aware of the physical requirements of the training he had just completed to get to where he was. For the courses he had to pass, he had trained extremely hard. I had watched him subject himself to tortuous runs, endure excruciating blisters, and carry around large weights in a backpack for hours at a time, all in a bid to be deprived of sleep every few weeks while pointing a firearm at someone. He told me that it was harder than he thought it would be. I pondered this. If he, as a capable male specimen, struggled, it didn't bode too well for me. Then he said something to me that changed things: 'You know, you could do it if you wanted to.'

It's funny how you can beat yourself up about your own failures, but when someone you admire and respect shows confidence in you, it changes your whole outlook. My husband and I have great respect and support for each other. We first met through policing, when I was two years senior to his junior-boy status (I try to take credit for all his good policing traits as being learnt from me). Through the years we have learnt each other's strengths and weaknesses, have seen each other through highs and lows, and gotten to know each other's capabilities. We also know each other's annoying habits. (I have none, but he peels his fingernails off and dumps them down the back of the couch. That's not nice.)

Up until then, I had only dabbled with the idea of applying for the AOS again as a kind of fantasy, never thinking it was possible. I mean, how would it fit in with my family's life now? Our son had grown and was just about ready for school. We had wonderful friends who were as much a part of our son's life as other family members were, and had always helped us out when my husband was away or had got called out. But AOS for both of us? This was a real lifestyle change. Was it manageable?

I needed to think this thing through. I knew I still wanted to do it; in fact, more than I had before. But my reasons now were different to my reasons back in 1998. In my day job I spent my time investigating serious crime, and although this was interesting and mentally challenging, spending so much time behind a desk investigating things wasn't really providing the excitement I needed. I knew that the AOS would complement my day job in this sense, but if I wanted to go ahead with it, there were lots of things to consider.

You know how when you're thinking of buying or selling a house, you make a 'list'? A list that shows all the pros and cons of whatever decision you make? Well, I did just that. I made myself a list for why I should, or shouldn't, apply.

...mit that it started off a bit crowded in the 'cons' corner. ...are that quite a few AOS members who had been in the ...ad left in recent years, so I hoped being a detective would ...be such a problem this time. But it was not something I could ...ank on. As well as this, I was not often 'on call' for CIB work due to child-care commitments — if a serious crime occurred, my number wouldn't be dialled often as there was a presumption I would be at home having to look after our son. I imagined that I would be criticised if I suddenly became able to go on call for a specialist squad such as the AOS. And having said that, was it actually possible? With my husband already on the squad, I couldn't exactly bring our child along with us on a call-out and leave him in the command vehicle with a squeaky toy.

Next, I was still not working full-time because of wanting to spend as much time as possible with our son while he was aged under five. I put 'only working part-time' down as a negative factor — despite the fact that our district had adopted strong EEO (Equal Employment Opportunities) and FEO (Flexible Employment Options) policies, there was only so far I was going to be able to push it. I did intend going back full-time when my little one started school, but even then I would still be working set hours to fit around schooling.

My husband being on the squad was something I thought was great, but I imagined that not everyone would share my happy view. Although I knew we had a great relationship and never argued (I kid you not), it would be difficult trying to convince everyone else of that.

My small size, and the perceptions of my capabilities based on that, would be some of the hardest issues to get past. I felt that those impressions had contributed to how far I'd got with my previous AOS applications. Whereas before I had always cashed in on my short stature within my chosen profession and the 'special' attention it brought me (as it wasn't always bad), this was not a time I wanted it. For the first time in my life, I wanted to be big.

When you conjure up an image of an AOS member, it's going to be an athletically built male who probably works out a bit, and is generally a lot fitter than most. I was none of that. Five foot two (just over 1.5 metres) and a weight under 60 kilograms might not cut it. There would be no dispensations for my size for this selection process. How would I physically deal with it? The three courses my husband had been required to complete before he was even allowed on the squad were intensely physical and more army-like than police-like, and from his description I knew they were certainly unlike anything I had ever done.

Then the pros. There were two; neither with any strong basis. First, my husband had told me I could do it and I was determined to live up to his expectations. Second, a recollection I had of a conversation some years previously with a male workmate who was also a serving AOS member back then. He had known that I was continually applying for the squad at the time, so it was with some surprise that I listened to his comments and 'words of wisdom' on the issue of females on the squad.

'Over my dead body will a female ever be on our AOS squad,' he proclaimed. I pondered his well-thought-out, well-articulated words that night and, indeed, in the following years. What was he trying to say to me? Was there a message there? No. He was actually just a chauvinistic tosspot. But his asinine comments nevertheless reinforced something in my head; and that something lay dormant and waiting over the years until finally bubbling to the surface in 2006. He had, in fact, given me a challenge. I rather like a challenge.

Having my husband's confidence in my ability foremost in my mind and the chauvinist's comment somewhere at the back, in September 2006 I decided, 'Bugger it. I'm going to do it,' and I threw my name in the hat along with five others.

3
PRE-SELECTION TRAINING

The AOS selection process had changed since I had originally tried to join in the 1990s. Now everyone, no matter who they were, was required to go through the same process regardless of their perceived potential as a future member of the squad. The old way was that a serving police officer would be approached by a member of the AOS and asked if they were interested. The approach would generally be based on having watched the potential applicant to see if they had the right qualities. Previous military – in particular army – experience was often an asset. The officer's name was then put forward to attend a selection and qualifying course, a three-week gut-busting extravaganza for the applicant to go through. From the stories, it focused on rather a lot of sleep deprivation.

The old way of selecting people did have its merits. The AOS is a tightly knit team that works in high-pressure situations and it would be detrimental to have a person on the squad that no one got on with; hence the reasoning that they should be allowed to pick their own. The new selection process also has its merits, however. It happens once a year, and goes like this:

1. Put your name forward to attend a District Selection course.
2. Attend District Selection (run over two days and one night).
3. Following successful completion and an interview, attend National Selection (three days and two nights).
4. Successful applicants attend a three-week qualifying course.

The selection courses are designed to give little or no break for sleep for the two or three days they run for, combined with many physical challenges. Under these conditions, instructors can see how you operate under fatigue and stress. Whether you like it or not, your true character comes through in a course like this and unsuitable people can thus be weeded out. If you were a plonker who couldn't make a decision if it came up and smacked you in the nose and said 'I'm a decision, come make me,' two intensely physical days with no sleep was going to make you stick out like the proverbial.

My first focus was, therefore, the district-level selection course. It was to be in March 2007 and was a slightly shorter version of the full National Selection course – two days instead of three. I began my training feeling the immediate hiccup of an old back injury I got from jumping out of an aeroplane in the early '90s and colliding with an aircraft hangar. Back then, I was young and foolish and thought parachuting was something everyone should do once. I was wrong. A cherry-picker had to pluck me from my perch, and I spent a lovely couple of days in hospital. I have learnt.

The District Selection course was seven months away, so my first two to three months of training were rehab work. It was about then that I found out that behind every strong woman are at least two stronger women – in my case, my physiotherapist and my massage therapist. I seemed to average two runs two days in a row, followed by three physio sessions and one massage session. I would stagger into these ladies' respective clinics, point out my ailments, the ladies would hammer me back into shape, and away I would go again.

My preparation consisted of running – lots of it – and selected weight-training exercises mostly using my own body weight, such as press-ups, pull-ups and sit-ups. I also wore pack weights, and hauled myself on two- and three-hour walks carrying anything between 10 and 25 kilos. I sweated and grunted my way through these chosen torture sessions every day, always visualising my end target – getting into the AOS. I even had a mantra as I walked: 'I'm gonna get into the AOS, I'm gonna get into the AOS.'

I did my best to fit my training in with as little disturbance to my family as possible – such as getting up very early, or incorporating my son into my pack walks; he'd sit in his buggy while his mother sweated all over the back of his head from above.

At that time, there had never been any females on the Central Districts Armed Offenders Squads – Central Districts encompassed Palmerston North (my home town), Wanganui and New Plymouth. I decided that as well as wanting to get on the squad for my own gratification, it would be a great coup for the girls. At that time in New Zealand there were only about four women on squads nationally.

My husband enthusiastically embraced my training regimen. He helpfully filled to the brim a backpack weed-sprayer one sunny Saturday, then sent me off up a rather elevated slope on our small Manawatu lifestyle block to spray weeds all day. Training, my arse – he was taking advantage of the situation and making me do a job he had no desire to do himself. He also found as many other back-breaking physical tasks as he could, assigning me those jobs with a wry smile.

But at the same time as I was grumbling, I was also relishing all the training. I have always loved a physical challenge, and to reach my first goal of passing District Selection I had been doing an exercise training programme specifically designed for getting through this course. Every day's activity that I wrote down as having been completed, I saw as one step closer to the standard of fitness I was required to reach. Before, if I felt the tiniest niggle of an injury or sneezed and had a slightly sore throat when I was training, I would call a halt to all exercise and have a week off. Now, nothing slowed me down. Surprisingly, the tiny niggles stayed tiny and the sore throat usually melted away into nothing.

If during weight-training I fleetingly thought about skipping the last set because I was feeling fatigued, I would think about the other applicants who were also training for this course. They would be training as hard, if not harder, than me. I didn't want them to do better than me just because I couldn't be bothered finishing my set exercises.

As training progressed, the runs got longer. Although I never went over 12 kilometres due to the fact that this often brought on injuries (I guess I'm not made for endurance), I would alternate a flat, fast 5-kilometre run with a slow, steady 12-kilometre grunt. At that time we lived on a large mountain range, so most runs would be up this.

Not being a very fast swimmer, I tried to spend more time in the pool even though I hated that part of the training. The only time I enjoyed it was when it followed a long run in the heat. Leaping into the cool depths of the outdoors pool was heavenly, although I struggled with the concept of which side to swim on. Never having swum in public pools (I was usually a 'leap in a round pool and splash around for a bit' kind of girl), I didn't know you had to stick to one side of the lane only. In my first couple of swims, I disrupted everyone by swimming on their side of the lane. My workmate screeched with laughter as I told her – with a mystified expression on my face – about the uppity people in the pool. She sang me lines from a Beyoncé Knowles song: 'To the left, to the left . . .' I imprinted this into my memory so that I wouldn't continue to offend. And for those who have no idea what I am talking about, when swimming in a lane pool you should always swim on the left-hand side. It saves embarrassment and head injury.

On another occasion I accidentally stole the swim club's lane and got kicked out; then, just when I thought I couldn't hate swimming any more than I already did, I had my car broken into and my phone and iPod stolen from it between the run and the swim. Luckily, the course was not far off now, so I only had a couple more weeks of enduring these torturous routines.

Once or twice a week, I would embark on a march with a weighted pack, acquiring blisters on each foot as I tried to figure out the best techniques to avoid them. As I set out, everything would feel fine; then the heat would begin in one area on my foot. I would halt and adjust my sock, but once it began it was difficult to stop. My hands were just as bad. As I walked up the hills on the hot days my fingers would swell up like cooked sausages, the skin straining at the knuckles when I tried to flex my fingers. I would try to walk with my arms in a cross over my chest, fingers hooked under the pack straps, to allow the fluid to drain away; but in the end I just had to put up with the feeling. I didn't imagine that they were likely to actually explode.

I also tried to tailor my training to what the situation would be on the course. I would always tramp in the boots I would be using and carry the weights we would have to carry on the course. Using the iPod while running was a fortnightly treat only (which ended after the pool theft, anyway), as I would not have the luxury of that distraction later on.

As time went by and people learnt what I was trying to achieve, I had a quote continually repeated to me: 'To be a woman in a man's world, you have to be twice as good to be half as good.' I have always subscribed to this in any physical tasks I have done, aiming to train at the boys' levels not the girls'. However, one day while waiting to get pummelled by my massage therapist, I found the same quote in a book in her waiting room. All the people who had quoted to me had, apparently, left out the end of it:

> To be a woman in a man's world, you have to be twice as good to be half as good. Luckily, this is not hard . . .

One day, this massage therapist gave me the greatest compliment I have ever received. It was close to the date of the selection course, and while merrily grinding the lactic acid out of my sore, tired muscles, she described how, 'As an athlete, you . . .' I have no recollection of the conversation other than this part of it, so impressed was I by being called an athlete. My chest swelled with pride at the thought of it. Up until that time, all the fitness ventures I had embarked on had been short-lived and mainly revolved around allowing me to eat more naughty foods and not put on any weight, or to pass the two-or-so-minute police PCT (physical competency test) every two years. This time round, however, I had trained specifically for getting through lots of hellish fitness tests. If I had applied the same dedication to my overeating formula that I had to my AOS training, perhaps I might have made the Olympics. Doing what, I have no idea. Preferably something you could sit down and eat at.

One nice, sunny day after work, close to the end of my training, I filled my backpack with lots of kilos of weight with the plan of walking home from the police station. I put on my trusted bike shorts, combat boots, and an old shirt. Thus attired, I swiped myself out of the station and started to head off. About 3 metres out of the front of the station, however, I heard yelling. I looked across the road to see an agitated man walking backward, waving his arms around and yelling obscenities. I looked to see who he was yelling at. One of the prosecuting police sergeants, who looked like he had just come from court, was strolling along at about the same pace as the backward-walking man, talking to him.

The man wasn't being very nice at all. I stopped and watched the spectacle for a few moments before throwing my backpack off and going to join the fun. I left the pack lying on the footpath outside the station perfectly confidently – anyone daft enough to steal it would have a surprise when they picked it up and tried to run off, as that day it weighed in at 30 kilos.

As I crossed the road, I saw that I wasn't the only one intrigued by what was happening. Other police officers had heard the yelling and had come out from the station. Seeing all the additional support, the prosecutor decided to instigate an arrest. He lunged forward and grabbed at the yeller, who threw a haymaker at him and turned to run off. As the yeller ducked behind a courier van that had stopped at the lights, the driver leapt out and joined in. By then I was there as well, and about four of us finally caught and jumped on the guy. I had his sharp end – his feet, which he was kicking out with – and was getting flapped around like a fish on a dry dock from the force of his kicks. My workmate Shelley appeared and, being the only one with handcuffs, she started to try to put them on him.

His shoes flew off, so now I had the equally horrid task of trying to hold his smelly feet. The courier driver had managed to get a couple of little jabs into the guy's ribs to slow him down, but he was still bucking and jerking and being wholly uncooperative. To my surprise, as I was being flung around I looked up to see a very well-known druggie, who had actually stopped and asked if he could help. I grunted out no thanks, and saw that he still stuck around, looking quite excited by the whole affair.

We finally managed to sit on a corner of the guy and, suitably flattened, he was able to be handcuffed at last. He was hauled to his feet and marched across to the station. I dusted myself off, picked out some small stones that had embedded themselves into the skin on my knees, and trotted back over to my backpack. Mission complete.

The next day, as I walked into the station I was greeted with, 'And here she is . . . Two Moons!' Shelley – the workmate who had turned up with the handcuffs – was regurgitating her version of events: racing out the front of the station and seeing two black Lycra-clad moons (my arse) pointing skyward and bouncing around all over the show while I was trying to restrain the guy. I laughed politely.

After the excitement of jumping on people while clad in Lycra, my final hurdle prior to starting the course was my overalls. For selection, we were all required to source our own sets of black AOS overalls from serving members. I had a pair left over from my PNT days, but I needed at least one or two more than this. No one had my size, though. I insulted the first two smaller squad guys I asked, who were put out that I would think they were that small. They were size 7 and 8, but I was a 3 or a 4. Finally, the district squad boss kindly allowed me to order a set in my size. As a joke (I hoped!) he forwarded the e-mail to another squad member (who wore size 10) along with the comment that if I failed, he would have to diet to fit mine so they weren't wasted.

AOS District Selection Course D-Day was 2 March 2007. It arrived sooner than expected, but by then I felt physically ready. I had only lost 2 kilos, which was probably about all I could spare due to not being a large-framed person, but that weight was the net result of lost body fat and gained muscle. I used the occasion to go on a shopping spree, as my CIB clothes all required pins to hold them up now.

I felt fit, strong and ready. I had got through a back injury, had acquired and got over an Achilles strain, and – regardless – had managed to build myself up to the highest standard of fitness I had ever reached, all at age 36. I felt quietly confident that I would survive the next two sleepless days and that I, now, would finally have a chance to prove myself.

4

LONELY DAYS AND SLEEPLESS NIGHTS

On the first day, as ordered, I turned up at the initial meeting point at Palmerston North police headquarters at 7.45 a.m., along with the five other hopefuls. My husband had taken time off work to keep the home fires burning and our wonderful friends were on stand-by in case the squad actually got a call-out. There was a slightly delayed start, though. The AOS had been called out on a job overnight, and as most of them were also tied up in the selection course, there was a bit of scrambling around to see who could peel away in time to torture us for the next two days. As a taste of things to come, perhaps, my husband hadn't gone on the job.

Our first test was a written one: one hour long on aspects of law relating to police use of firearms, and use of force. I had known of this component beforehand and had spent the previous couple of weeks adding a bit of study into my day while tapering off my physical regimen. I went through the test, confident that my study had been sufficient to allow me to pass. Straight after this, as they marked our tests, we were lined up and began what would turn into 36 hours on the go.

We started by running for about half an hour, stopping for

press-ups and burpees (a squatting movement followed by a rear-thrusting leg movement), then lined up for an RFL (Required Fitness Level test). This involved running 2.4 kilometres within a certain time-frame, followed by a set number of press-ups. I snuck in just on time, with only one other person in front of me. So far, so good.

We got our first reaming-out then. As we were lined up, the assigned instructor marched up and down our line. 'We've just marked the tests. If we were doing this by the book, there would only be two of you left here. That's fucking pathetic! If you think you've come along for a laugh, then I suggest you leave . . .' That sort of ranting. I kept looking down at the ground in front of me, not wanting to be the object of his anger. After a while, the tirade died down and we were off again.

We did yet more press-ups as punishment for being 'so fucking useless', then we ran for another half-hour or so, this time with a medicine ball carried between us. Damn ball weighed half a tonne. It was red, and pretty obviously designed to 'test our mettle' as a team. As we ran, we passed it around, keeping up an encouraging banter between us.

We ran across Palmerston North, ending up on the far side of town. Then we did the PCT – first you run over a 400-metre track, then you jump over things, under things and through things, and then drag things, all within a set time. With the AOS, your times have to be faster than what is normally required for general policing.

Prior to starting the PCT, I could feel that my feet were already beginning to blister. It wasn't because I was doing anything harder than I had done in my training, but I had just learnt my first valuable lesson – if you're going to tape feet and toes to prevent blisters, make sure you tape all of them.

After I'd finished my run and PCT I had a few minutes to wait while the rest of the applicants went through, so I quickly checked my feet. They weren't very pretty to look at. Unfortunately, with the

12 or so kilometres we had already run, the untaped toes had rubbed on the taped ones, taking thick layers of my skin with them. They were red, raw, and bleeding in parts. This wasn't a very good start.

We then had the swimming phase. This was the most detested part of the course for me, if I am to be brutally honest. With all the training I was fit and not too flabby, but I didn't fancy for one second parading around in my swimsuit in front of a bunch of male AOS members. While they all sat around watching the applicants and noting our teamwork, general attitudes and physical capabilities, I had to endure the humiliation of wandering around in front of them wearing a swimsuit that, after I'd swum half a length, always seemed to end up embedded in my bum cheeks like a G-string. Which is great for the beach at Surfers Paradise where no one cares what my bum looks like – least of all me – but not so flash in the pool in Palmerston North in front of an audience of 10.

I swam my way up and down the pool for the set number of lengths (trying to do as few leg movements as possible to minimise the swimsuit creep), dived for a brick, then dragged a course-mate up the pool (and was dragged in return). Every second that my hands were free, I tugged and pulled at my swimsuit to get it back into order.

After passing the required tests, I was allowed to get out of the pool and, finally, into the aimed-for black overalls. So far we had only worn PT (physical training) gear. Putting on the overalls on this occasion made me feel the way I did the first time I put on a police uniform: immensely honoured and very privileged. I was brought back to earth within five minutes, though. We were slow getting changed after getting out of the pool, so were punished with shuttle runs.

But things were still going well. We had been threatened with getting dropped if we failed anything, and I was quietly confident I hadn't. Despite the fact that we'd been told most of us had failed the written test, etc., etc., I believed my test had been a pass. I also knew my first tested run was a pass, and so was the PCT. Mind-games were obviously a component of these two days. I didn't start to think ahead to what was next, though – I just concentrated on getting through one task at a time. As one would expect, we were all competing against each other for a spot on the squad, so although we had to act as a team, we also had to be competitive in the testing areas that were pass/fail.

As well as the black overalls, we were required to wear training body armour everywhere we went. It was about the same weight as operational body armour – the ballistic vest or body armour that police officers wear when attending any armed incident – but this training one had a non-ballistic inner (i.e. it wouldn't stop bullets), and was red without any police insignia. Having not worn body armour before for any length of time, I found it cumbersome and heavy.

The rest of the course activities began to blur at about this point. During my pre-course training, I had continually annoyed my husband by probing him for information about what was going to be happening. 'I can't remember,' he used to say. I couldn't fathom how he could forget such a momentous occasion in his life, but now, after having gone through it myself, I do. With the lack of sleep and the heavy physical component you are utterly exhausted, and thinking back you can't remember whole segments, or what order they occurred in. Chances are very high that I'll be muddling the order of events I'm relating to you now, such was my tiredness by the end – but rest assured, the content is accurate enough.

As I already had that first wad of blisters on my feet following the morning's beating, whenever I ran or walked anywhere I was continually reminded that this was just the beginning. We were taken out to a warehouse next, where we were to be put through some 'shoot/don't shoot' scenarios. Part-way there, we were kicked out of the van and made to run for a couple of kilometres, of course wearing the body armour. Why? What had we done? Nothing – it was 'just because'.

One of the hardest components of this course was actually not knowing anything about what you were going to be doing. One moment you could be standing around waiting, the next you would be told to start running. Once you started running, you didn't know when you would be told to stop. You also didn't know how much to push yourself, as who knew what would be next? It was this exact scenario that gauged mental strength.

The only light-hearted moments on the course were during travel time. The two guys who were acting as our course staff were also our taxi drivers. Aside from telling us timings and the like, they provided no forms of encouragement, but as they revved the van through the gears one of them would make that infuriating hiss that boy racers' cars make when they're burning around suburban streets at 3 a.m. While taking care not to draw attention to ourselves with loud laughter at their playful foolishness, it was a welcome, light-hearted relief.

The shoot/don't shoot exercises involved scenario-based training that tested your decision-making ability. You were told the scenario, then pretty much left to deal with it. The offender was played by another cop who, notoriously, had been given a different briefing to you – such as: if the police officer shows weakness, exploit it. Such weakness could be indecisiveness, lack of control of the situation, or inability to follow the law in the use of firearms.

My scenarios were pretty weak in terms of demonstrating my ability to 'dominate'. For one of them, I was briefed that I was approaching the scene as a lone cop, back-up was an hour away, and therefore it was just me. My (wrong) approach was to negotiate my way out of it – ask/tell/make the baddie do what you wanted. This means ask them first, and if they refuse then tell them, and if they still refuse then make them. I should have adopted make/make/make. In the AOS, they have people who negotiate; they are called negotiators. I wasn't meant to be doing that. In fact, I had already done that as a job, so, out of everyone, I should have known better. Most of my scenarios were resolved okay – in that I didn't get shot. However, I knew that my soft approach would be criticised later.

We were given FX – 'simmunition' (the equivalent of paint balls). The firearm we used was a Glock (the small handgun that police in New Zealand use), and these training Glocks were specially adapted for FX ammo. It added reality to the situation, as you would be able to actually shoot the villain, and in turn you could find out how good or bad you were at cover and concealment when he or she shot you back.

One scenario that I can vividly recall involved getting grabbed and pushed into a room without any briefing about what I was going to confront; I just had to cope. As soon as I entered the room, a bunch of hysterical role-players grabbed at me, screaming at me to help them and distracting me from god knew what. Then, while I was suitably distracted, 'god knew what' popped out from behind a wall and basically drilled me with FX. The gunman role-player, a current AOS member, aimed specifically for areas where I wasn't covered by protective gear – the thighs and groin. It was hard to concentrate, especially as when I shot the first round off I was being hit in said nether regions, then had a weapon malfunction while still getting drilled. I tried to take cover to fix my weapon without getting constantly nailed, but the exercise supervisor tried to push me back out into the fray.

FX rounds leave a nice red welt the size of a 50 cent piece, which is surrounded by a fist-sized bruise (or bigger if you're susceptible to bruising). The pain on impact is quite sharp; it feels like someone has pinched you really hard. They can do a lot of soft-tissue damage, which is why protective head, chest, and in particular eye gear is a must when doing any exercise involving FX. I came out of the 'room of chaos' exercise looking like I'd fallen thigh-first on bright red and green marker pens.

Following another exercise, I was led off to sit alone in a darkened passageway. There, I had to write out, word for word, one of the firearms regulation sections. This was my 'down time'. As I sat there I could hear a monotonous, droning voice, followed by a beep. It would be silent for a bit, then it would happen again. Same voice, same drone, same beep. *Ahh, Chinese torture*, I thought. *That actually sounds quite restful.* After about 15 minutes of listening to this, I was told 'Follow me', and was led through to another area.

The whole of this section of scenarios took place in a disused abattoir (later condemned because of asbestos), so the rooms we were in were huge, dusty (in hindsight, probably asbestos dust) and dirty, but empty. I was wearing my black overalls, boots and ballistic vest. I was led into a massive room to another instructor, and was told that I was now to do a beep test. I had often heard about sportspeople doing beep tests, but don't recall ever having had the pleasure myself. It involves running between two set points, and you have to reach each end prior to the next beep. As you progress, the beeps get closer together. So *that* was the noise I had been listening to. There would be no rest, then.

At 'Go!', I began to run back and forth in my overalls, boots and body armour. At first, when I got to each end I would stop and catch my breath, but as time went on the gaps between the beeps lessened and I had to start running a bit faster. I had no idea how long I was to run for. I was wishing I'd paid more attention when I'd heard people talking about beep tests. As my shuffles became jogs, then my jogs became runs, then my runs became sprints, I was getting more and more tired; then, unexpectedly, when I reached 10 I was told to stop. A gas mask was thrust into my hand, I was given a Glock containing FX, and was told to 'deal with the scenario'. With heightened pulse rate, tiredness, and now the infernal gas mask on, I immediately fogged up and couldn't see anything. I blindly followed the sound of the instructor's voice.

I was directed toward a large room. It looked like it had been one of the many slaughter rooms used when the place was a freezing works; I hoped that the slaughter theme wasn't going to continue with me today. There was an opening to the far left of the side I was facing, and from where I was entering, the room widened out to the right. Instead of leaping straight into the room, I sheltered to the right of the opening and listened. That was what I was being tested for – was I going to leap in, expose myself and get shot, or was I going to use common sense in my approach?

On cue, while I was waiting and listening, inside a woman began screaming. I carefully manoeuvred myself so that with each shuffle, a little more of the room was revealed, and with firearm raised and pointing where my eyes were looking, I finally saw, sitting facing me in the far left corner of the room, a woman. She was screaming hysterically, and to her left was a male with a sawn-off shotgun. He was holding her hostage.

After a short attempt at negotiation – which ended when he raised his gun at me – I shot him. With the woman still screaming at me to help her, I tried to get her to come to me. I wasn't going to enter the room, as I sensed a trap. But she wouldn't get up. She just sat there, screaming and pleading with me to help her. Realising that she wasn't going to come to me, I instructed her to hide in the corner where she was, then – still without entering the room – I tried to get a better view of the far right corner, which was still hidden from me. A whizzing and popping sound of FX rounds coming at me said it wasn't quite safe to enter.

A second offender was hiding behind an obstacle in that corner of the room, and any time I tried to poke my head around the corner to figure out where he was hiding, he shot at me. After much to-ing, fro-ing, popping and whizzing, he finally came out and surrendered to me. 'End ex!' was called – the cue that the exercise had ended. I did a quick body check . . . so far, so good. No hits. The guy I'd plugged in the left corner of the room had a decent welt on his stomach, however. He was our medic, and I was glad I hadn't managed to shoot any of his helping hands. I still had blisters I needed him to fix.

The 'down time' activity I was talking about earlier – the writing out of general instructions on the use of firearms – was a real pain. The law is under police General Instructions (GIs), and is called F61 and has to be known verbatim. In its entirety it's about 600 words long. When you're tired, you get unsure and second-guess things — *I think that's what it says, but have I muddled the bits up again?* I'd scribble bits out, then try to write them again, knowing I was forgetting more as time went on. We also had to do Sudoku. Ah, Sudoku. I'd never done it before in my life. I wasn't going to ask what to do because I didn't want to bring any attention upon myself unnecessarily, and if its intention was just to keep me busy then perhaps they wouldn't check it anyway. So, having no idea what I was supposed to be doing, I just randomly wrote down lots of numbers in the empty boxes. At least I looked like I was keeping busy.

We kept on the move until about 7 p.m. on this first day. Then, after a quick scoff of some freeze-dried delicacy, we were told to make sure any blisters were sorted. What was our next surprise to be? It could be team building, it could be an hour-long run, it could be more Sudoku . . . I had no way of knowing.

To give you an idea of what the feeling of not knowing is like, stop reading for a minute (after this paragraph) and put yourself in this space. Imagine turning up for work having been told to bring in a pair of running shoes and some sports gear. Half an hour into the day, you get told to put the shoes on and line up. Then you're told to run, so you do. The route you are told to take is haphazard and doesn't seem to have any end point. You know this run could be you for the whole day. Equally, it could end around the next corner; but you know you've still got seven hours of the workday left, and it could go for that long. If you don't have any options but to keep going, could you? Do you push yourself, or leave a little in the tank? How hard could it actually get?

I thought of my husband a lot. I imagined he was dreading a phone call saying could he come and pick me up — 'She's done — she couldn't keep up.' I was only just now appreciating what he had gone through two years previously.

My blisters were by now very sore, but they were made even worse when the medic assigned to the entire two-day course poured iodine onto them that first night. He assured me it was meant to help them — antiseptic or something — but it felt more like a form of torture. He may have been getting me back for the gut shot. After getting sorted as best as I could, we headed off in minivans to the Tararua Ranges. For a nice wee stroll. Yeah, right.

Between the six of us we were given a number of heavy objects, one of which was a wooden box containing about 20 kilos of something heavy (I think it was sand), and we began to walk. And we walked, and we walked, and we walked. Up a great big hill. Through a gate. Down some dips. Up more hills. As well as carrying the assortment of cumbersome objects, we were still wearing body armour, which was not exactly like a second skin. My body armour was uncomfortable and restrictive. It sat too low, so when walking uphill my thighs would hit against the bottom of the armour, limiting my leg movements. It rubbed on any of my bony bits — mainly my collar-bone and shoulders. I somehow managed to keep all my moaning and swearing within the confines of my head.

When we got to the top of a great big hill, we found that we were now only five — one of the team had been plucked off the back of the group where they had ended up. Unfortunately, the staff didn't take the object that team-mate had been carrying, so now we had one more item to share between five of us instead of six. Ever aware that at any time we could be the next one to get kicked off for not keeping up, we then walked down the big hill. And when we got to the bottom of the big hill, we kept walking. Finally we stopped. Mercifully, all our equipment was taken off us and we were told to get in the minivans. But I smelled a rat. No sooner had we closed the van door than we were told to get out. Rodney the rat had shown up.

A 'casualty' was down the road and we had to go down to them, put them on a stretcher (which was conveniently beside the person — how handy), and carry them forward to an RV (rendezvous) point some distance away. It sounded straightforward enough, until I saw that the casualty was Darrell, an old friend of mine. He had been playing the bad guy in a few scenarios earlier in the day, and as a result of how well he had played his role I was a bit sick of the sight of him. He wasn't light, and I groaned at the thought of lugging his carcass for an indeterminate distance.

I was given the role of team leader. As there were five of us, we had four carrying the stretcher at any one time with the fifth walking alongside, and we continually rotated. It sounds pretty straightforward and easy, but it was tough. When SAR (Search and Rescue) does a stretcher-carry, they do it with something like a minimum of eight holding the stretcher. By now we had been on the go since 9 a.m. that morning, and it was getting close to 1 a.m. We had barely stopped moving the whole time, although I wasn't sure just how many kilometres we had clocked up. My guesstimate was 'lots'. We were knackered. The heavy end was the head. Being the weakest of the four of us, I was fortunate to be able to call changes in our positions when 'I' needed it. We continued to rotate around the stretcher in a clockwise direction, with the fifth person keeping an eye on the 'patient'.

We'd got to about our fifth rotation on the stretcher when we started to get yelled at. When we rotated we had to stop to change positions, and I would use the guise that the 'patient' needed to be monitored to give everyone a quick break. This didn't take long to get noticed — and stomped on. 'Get fucking moving! You're only going to the top of that hill! Fucking get a move on and stop fucking about!' Duly noting the suggestion — and now knowing how far we had to go — we stopped fucking about and dragged ourselves up the next hill, where we were finally allowed to put the stretcher down. I felt like kicking Darrell.

We eventually all got back into the vans and sat there meekly and quietly while we were taken back to our base, which was the Palmerston North Police Dog Base. By now it was 1.30 a.m. It was a bit strange seeing the gear for the team-mate who had left all still laid out there. I did, however, take advantage of an opportunity and stole all their bananas.

Most of us now had blister problems that the medic sorted again, then we were allowed to sleep. We had roll-mats and sleeping bags and were to sleep on the floor of the dog base. Excellent. I had also brought ear plugs along, and no sooner had I put them in than I fell into a deep slumber.

My slumber took me to 4 a.m. when I was woken by bright lights and one of the instructors telling us to get up while he cheerfully made himself a cuppa. The worst thing when you're tired is cheery, awake people. I wanted to pour his cuppa over his head then ram the cup that had held the liquid up an orifice of his.

The AOS guys who ran the course – whom we referred to as 'staff' – were not allowed to engage us in friendly chit-chat. It seemed strange at the onset – I had known some of them for years – but like all the other applicants there, I didn't want anyone to accuse me of special treatment through acting too familiarly.

We were told to get into our blacks (black overalls), and be outside in five minutes. Knowing from the previous day's shuttle runs how important timing was, we all rushed about getting sorted and lined up outside. Sitting on the ground in front of us were five army backpacks. I grimaced at the thought of what they weighed.

Our instructions were then barked at us in true military fashion. We were to put on the backpacks and complete a BET (Battle Efficiency Test). It was a 12-kilometre walk, which was to be completed in under 1 hour 50 minutes and was to be done carrying a 25-kilo backpack. Yippee. We were given the course route around the streets of Palmerston North, but, I must confess, I didn't listen all that well because I couldn't stop staring at the backpack. As with everyone else, after two hours of sleep, bad blisters and physical exhaustion from the day and night's exercise before, I knew the next couple of hours would be hard.

When I had done my training, I had carried weights in a backpack, but had used a Gucci-style (meaning a fancy pansy kind, rather than real Gucci – do they actually make packs?), super-comfy one, which had lots of straps, padding and support. It was also a very nice colour. This one was camouflage, steel-framed and moulded to someone who was an entirely different shape to me. This was gonna hurt.

As soon as I hoisted the ill-fitting, 25-kilo army backpack up, I knew I was going to struggle and a spontaneous feeling of hopelessness and dread came over me. The fact that I was thinking failure thoughts and I hadn't yet started walking was a concern. I had 12 kilometres in front of me, I was exhausted, my feet hurt a lot, and my pack was immediately rubbing on my back even before I took a step. The shoulder straps were too long and caused me to practically lean backward with the weight, but as we were getting hurried along I didn't have time to shorten them. Luckily one of the staff noticed, and with two efficient tugs at the straps the pack closed in against my back, providing an instantly better fit.

But it did hurt. With staff yelling at us to hurry up, away I went. We were let off at two-minute intervals, with the trick being not to let the person behind pass you. I took off at a good pace on the wrong side of the road. This was corrected when I hit the first intersection and was told to cross to the other side.

The pack rubbed. My feet rubbed and I had chafing. I felt like throwing up. I was not a happy troopie. I sucked back a liquid supplement I had brought with me, in an attempt to keep my energy levels up, but when I put the wrapper back in my pocket like the tidy Kiwi I was, the dregs soaked through my overalls, which then stuck to my leg. So I tried my mantra to get me 'in the zone' and out of the grumpy mood I felt myself falling into.

'I want to be in the AOS. I want to be in the AOS. I want to be in the AOS. No I fucking don't! This sucks. I need sleep! No! Stuff them! I do want to do this. Or do I?! Stupid fucking damn sticky supplement packet!'

As I walked, I was mystified as to where the others who'd gone ahead of me were. I hadn't seen anyone. We had to walk the first 6 kilometres out on one side of the road and walk back on the other, but I must have been so 'in my zone' that I hadn't seen anyone. Surely someone had passed me somewhere? At one point, I turned off too early and started heading down one street too soon. I was yelled back into line, and imagined them putting a cross next to my name. 'Williams. That's a fail for not listening to simple instructions . . .'

During the last 4 kilometres, I had a quick look behind me and saw one of the fitter guys bearing down on me. He was running. *Running?* How the hell he ran I had no idea. Not wanting to be outdone and passed, I did some version of running; it was more of a shuffle in a forward direction. I tried to keep ahead, but after a short struggle he overtook me. 'Keep it going, Lizzy Bizzy,' he cheerfully told me as he jogged past. So he was fit *and* happy! What an arse! I shuffled to keep up with him for as long as I could. I probably lasted about 1 kilometre, but he was too strong for me.

Every now and then the instructors would cruise past in a van. They never said anything; the van would run alongside me for a few metres, then would fall back or roar ahead, but whenever it was around I would see the occasional flash of a camera. In my tiredness I though it was a torch and they were trying to distract me with it, so I made a point of ignoring them.

But 1 hour and 42 minutes later, I was done. *Woo hoo!* I was elated to be finished. *Now* I didn't feel too bad. Then I was told to fireman's-carry my team-mate (Mr Happy, who weighed 86 kilos) 100 metres up the road. As I hoisted him up over my shoulder, I let out an expletive in disgust at his weight – not that he could do anything about it. I staggered the whole way, dropping him about a centimetre over the finish line.

Following this, I had to leap over a 2-metre wall (without carrying anyone), which my now-jelly legs got me through; then we had a blissful hour and a half to shower, sort blisters and eat. It was a lovely, lovely break and, best of all, I now had 24 hours of the course behind me.

The rest of the day consisted of further scenarios, a bit more getting yelled at, then problem-solving exercises. These exercises were the type where you are given a pair of gumboots (pink ones) and, within your team, have to get everyone across a 'swamp' filled with crocodiles, with each person crossing in the boots only once. From memory (just in case you get landed with the same exercise some time in your life), the trick is to have your biggest team-mate make the first trip carrying two across the 'swamp'.

Strangely enough for me, in the problem-solving exercises I seemed to have these moments of clarity where the answer unfolded before my eyes. One exercise involved sticky tape, kebab skewers and a water bottle. We had to build a bridge and balance the bottle on it as proof of its sturdiness. I wasn't very good at bridges. Knowing that too many hands can overcomplicate things, after beginning the process of sticking our bridge together I sat back and let another team member have a go. As he was trying to tape the bits together, I watched in frustration as his big chipolata fingers crushed bits of the bridge, generally making a big mess, and finally I could contain myself no longer.

'For god's sake, let me do that! Your great big sausage fingers are wrecking it! No one is ever going to want you on *Play School* with skills like that!' I took over, using my little girly fingers to nimbly stick together our abortion of a bridge. I later heard that, from a distance, one of the instructors had heard my raised voice and had thought I'd actually lost it. He obviously hadn't heard the content of the conversation.

Later in the day we were taken down for an exercise in a tunnel. I had heard of these tunnels before – just never been in them. They were in the Massey University compound and went for some distance under the university, carrying pipes and the like from one side of the campus to another.

After we arrived, one by one the group members were led off to their tunnel exercise, finally leaving me alone at the van. I lay back, shut my eyes and, as best as I could, relaxed. I was just about to nod off when I heard approaching footsteps, so quickly sat up, trying to look awake and alert.

Still trying to wake myself up, I was taken to the tunnel entrance and given a brief. A security guard from the university had been down in the tunnel with another security guard, chasing some suspicious males. The offenders had shot at the guards. One had managed to escape and call the police, but there still was one guard unaccounted for. I was handed a set of ear plugs, but, wanting to hear the rest of the briefing, I didn't put them in straight away.

As I was led down to the scenario, I was told that I had two others to assist me: two of my course-mates who had already completed the scenario. I took on the role of leading them in, then was told I had to wear a gas mask to carry out the 'mission' – that of locating and retrieving the lost guard.

Donning the cumbersome mask, I led the other two down the tunnel. As we cleared the first part of the hallway, my ears were suddenly blasted into the next day by a shotgun blank going off up ahead. I had, of course, forgotten to put my ear plugs in. I'd seen the flash and, with ears still ringing, crept ahead to what seemed to be an inert form on the floor further down the tunnel. As I neared it I was shot at again, so let rip with a couple of return blanks, causing further havoc to my eardrums. My two offsiders were directly behind me, so, going slightly forward of the motionless form, I directed them to uplift the victim and drag him back up the tunnel to where we'd come from. The 'victim' was actually a 70-kilo dummy that we used for dragging during our physical competency tests.

'No, no, you drag him and we'll cover you,' I was told. I *don't think so*, I thought. I wasn't sure what the focus of this exercise actually was – I hadn't been told I was the team leader or anything, but my telling the other two (who had been through the scenario already) what to do seemed like the logical thing.

'You drag him and I'll cover,' I told them again. Again, they tried to insist that I do the dragging, but I stubbornly refused. Creeping backward with my eyes on the murky tunnel ahead of us, I could hear the scraping of the motionless dummy as it was dragged up the incline toward the entrance.

As we rounded the last corner, 'End ex' was called. We all ripped off our masks, were directed out, and told to wait at the van again. As we walked back, I rubbed my face where the tight-fitting mask had cut in and shook my head to try to get my ears working again. 'Did you know you were meant to drag the dummy?' one of the guys who had done the exercise with me asked.

'I thought with the three of us there, and you having already done the scenario, I had to act as a leader or something,' I told him, slightly confused.

'After we'd done the exercise, they told us the purpose of it was for testing stress while wearing the gas mask in a confined space, with the addition of physical exertion – dragging the dummy,' he told me.

'Whoops,' I said. The poor guy had had to drag the 70-kilo lump 100 metres up an incline twice then – once for himself, and the second time with me bossing him around. All in all, I came out of it very lightly!

As the afternoon dragged on, we were given a navigation exercise, and set off in a team of three. I'm not sharp at navigation at the best of times, and getting lost in the streets of Palmerston North didn't feel like a good way to end the day. We didn't know when the day would end, either. Would we still be here at 8 p.m.? With no way of knowing the end time, we wandered around the streets with our maps. It was a stinking-hot day, so we all took in as much fluid as we could handle. A couple of times we decided to walk, but that soon changed when a police vehicle carrying an instructor cruised around the corner, clearly keeping an eye on us. With blisters stinging at every step, we kept jogging/shuffling, completed the exercise and handed our maps in with, hopefully, the right answers.

Then we lined up for yet more running. In our group of five with the instructor running to one side, we set off to god knew where. There were mind-games, when you thought you were ending the run but then you'd continue past where you'd thought you might be stopping, but I had gone beyond the point of caring. I knew that it would end that night, so what was another couple of hours? The worst part was actually stopping for any length of time, at a set of lights or to wait for one of the group to catch up. The blisters would start to sting; then, when you set off running again, they would rub afresh.

As we ran up a street that led to the police station, a couple of guys in the group remarked that there was the station and we were nearly there. *Nope*, I thought. *There's still daylight* . . . but then, miracle of miracles, we were done! Our instructor ran us into the station yard and down to the AOS room.

'Gun cleaning now. Sort out your cleaning equipment and get to it.'

So that was it? We were allowed to finish? We were clearly all tickled pink with what we'd achieved, and a bit of hand-shaking and back-slapping went on, but we were also pretty tired and exhausted. We still had one of the staff with us, so weren't ready to let down our guard just yet.

We went back to dog base by van. As we pulled in, I saw my husband and my little five-year-old boy. He was ready to sprint up to me to give me a cuddle, but was stopped by my husband – it wasn't quite all over yet. I smiled and waved at them instead.

We were treated to a barbecue (cooked by my husband), and I was finally able to give the family a hug. During the barbecue, we spoke quietly within our group – it was still really *them* and *us* – serving AOS guys who had been our instructors, and us wannabes. We then underwent an individual debrief. One of the first things we were told to do was to rate ourselves in the order we thought we had finished in. It was a bit embarrassing, really. All of us had been through an ordeal together that we felt a strong bond from. We had now seen each other at our best and our worst, and to put one ahead of the other was hard. I scribbled down my answer, handing my paper back while hoping it would never be referred to again as long as I lived.

When asked what I thought I hadn't done well in, I brought up my lack of dominance. I was quizzed a lot on this, which isn't surprising when you consider the role of the AOS. Finally, I was allowed to go. After a few farewells, we went home. I risk sounding like a big-head – and trust me, I'm not – but I was extremely proud of what I'd achieved in the two days. I wasn't so proud of my lack of dominance during scenarios, but I knew that if I was allowed to proceed, I would work on this. I knew what I had to do differently.

I got my course report a few days later. 'Showed intestinal fortitude', was the quote I'll always remember. And here was me thinking I'd left my intestinal fortitude at the top of the Tararua Ranges.

In my bid to get on the AOS I now had one course down, but there were still two to go. The first two courses were entirely up to me to achieve – the passing was based on my physical and mental aptitude. Selection to go on the last course, however, was a decision that I felt would be down to politics. I felt this for all the reasons I'd put on my 'cons' list. Ultimately, and regardless of anyone else's opinion as to my worthiness, someone who gets paid far more than me would have to decide whether, even if I had performed to the required standards, I was going to progress to the final stage.

The next few weeks were an anticlimax after the ferocity of the course. I didn't train at all, letting my blisters and my body heal. The next course date was set for 13 May – Mother's Day and also the day after my birthday. When training, it's good to have a goal to train toward. Unfortunately, they didn't confirm who was on the course for a whole month after the first one. My training was, therefore, rather unfocused. I had also lost two toenails, so used this as an excuse to put my feet up.

But then I got the word – I was through to the next round! National Selection, here I come!

5

NATIONAL SELECTION

With my husband adapting his work shifts around sole child-care responsibilities for the next few days, I finally set off on National Selection. I crapped myself all the way down to Police College in Porirua. I was so nervous. One night with limited sleep hadn't been much fun and this was two nights, plus you could pack a lot more exercise into three days. I also knew that I wasn't as fit this time. I was full of flu and had a bad cough that I'd nursed for the previous two weeks, which hadn't been assisted greatly by training. Three of us from Palmerston North had been passed for National Selection and this year it had been split into two courses, running one week after another. I would be travelling down with only one of the Palmy guys, as the other applicant had been down the week previously — and had survived!

We hadn't asked him what went on and he probably wasn't allowed to tell us all the details, but I found that I didn't want to know too much anyway. I was still going to have to do it, regardless of what I knew about it.

On the way down with the other Palmy guy, we did last-minute study quizzes as he drove. When we got there, I got my key and headed to where I was to be staying. The College accommodation consists of blocks of flats with lots of floors, each floor having six rooms on it and communal showers and toilets. When I'd dragged my bags up to my floor, I saw I was sharing it with five blokes. There were 32 on the course, and I was to be the only female.

While no one voiced any opinions to me, I felt very conspicuous in my nice pink top and with my hair in a ponytail. I was lugging two huge roll-bags up the stairs, full of pilfered, begged and borrowed AOS kit as well as a few personal items that I could save for the end. As I climbed the three flights of stairs, I tried to make the bags I was carrying look like they were featherweight – no mean task when they were about 25 kilos each. Common sense would have said take two trips. Stubbornness said I could do it in one.

As I passed what seemed like floor after floor of large, buffed, fit-looking prospective AOS blokes, I grunted out to ask if this was the AOS course. I was regarded with barely concealed surprise. I looked more like I should have been on the photography course that was being run at the same time.

When you're in unknown territory, you look for some familiar ground. Just one female face would have been nice, but it wasn't to be. As I hope you realise by now, I'm not the kind of woman who has to shun all females when trying to tackle a bloke's domain – I don't need to be a boy to fit in with boys, and I also don't just hang out with lots of boys so I can score one or five. Over the years I've met a few ladies like this, and it really gets under my skin. You know the kind – they treat you like competition: you might steal the attention of one of the 40 blokes they formerly 'had to themselves'. I don't think it's a good look. A friendly smile of acknowledgement from someone of the same sex, simply because they are the same sex, would be nice to make you feel welcome. So bring on the girls, I say – the more, the merrier.

I later learned that the only other female attending National Selection had been on the course the week before, and she, like me, was the only woman among 32 applicants. I had yet to meet her and I wished she was here now; but she wasn't, so I would just have to cope.

We applicants unpacked and met each other, learning that some had been on squads already for a few months, either just being the dogsbody or going to AOS training days. I had done none of that. I was familiar with a lot of AOS practices from my negotiating days, but was in the dark about most of the skills and drills the AOS used when they went forward.

On my floor, one of the guys paraded around in his little undies, telling me that he hoped I wouldn't be offended but he would probably do worse further into the three days. He wasn't too awful to look at, so I let him get away with it. In my experience, partial nakedness has always been an excellent ice-breaker.

Our first briefing was on the Sunday night. After a mess meal, we all met up outside a classroom. Once again, I felt conscious of surreptitious once-overs from the rest of the blokes, who weren't on my floor so didn't even know me a little. If I'd been a mind-reader, my guess would have been: 'This will be interesting. I can't see her making it through the first night.' I suddenly felt hideously uncomfortable and obvious.

Apart from one guy who recognised me from when we were in the Air Force together (a previous life-experience during which I painted aeroplanes and packed life-rafts), no one sought out my witty conversation and introduced themselves to me, so I just stood there, trying to blend in. When we were finally allowed in the classroom, introductions were made by the instructors, we were told the course layout and timings, and were given the written test to do. This was the same set-up as at District, with one hour to complete it, and the test covering all the laws on use of force and F61 requirements. I had studied the material thoroughly prior to the course, and was damn sure I wouldn't get kicked off on the first day. After finishing it, I was again confident that I had passed. We then had individual photos taken, and were given a series of lessons in knot tying. Throughout the course, these knots were to be our new version of Sudoku – something to never let us relax. At least this time they would be useful.

We were also given bright-red bibs with numbers on, and for the next three days I was to be known as Number Five. The bib was to be worn everywhere and reduced our identity to that of a number, not a person. We were also given our new best friend – a 'rebar', more commonly known as a reinforcing bar, which was in effect just a length of metal roughly the same size and weight as a long firearm. The weight of a real operational firearm varies depending on whether it has a muzzle suppressor and/or a full magazine on at the time; it could be between 4 and 8 kilos. These rebars weighed about 5 kilos and were to be carried with us everywhere in the same manner as you would carry a firearm. One end had a bit of tape around it – this was the business end. We weren't to drop it, and heaven help the person who forgot muzzle safety – never point it in the wrong direction: you could take an eye out with one of those things.

Along with the others, I joylessly took charge of the old army backpack that was to hold all the kit we would need for whatever the day's activities promised – swimming gear, running gear, and walking gear. We would need to carry this pack with us everywhere as well.

Once we had received the list of all the things the pack should contain, we gathered everything together and spread it over the floor so it could be checked. Gas mask, wet-weather gear, thermals, and swimming gear, to name a few. The bag I had brought with me to hold my swimming gear was a maroon number, with a bright cartoon picture of a bikini top and bottom on one side. When packing to come down, I had told my husband I was going to take it. 'Don't be stupid,' he said. 'You'll look like an idiot. It's an AOS course, not a Girl Guides' camp.' But I stubbornly thought I would anyway. This is what girls used when they went swimming, and I was a girl.

Now I felt like a fool. He had been right. Among all the khaki, black and brown lay my decorated maroon toilet bag for all to see. I kicked it underneath my pack. What an idiot.

We were broken up into four sections of eight. We then had all of our watches and cellphones taken off us, rendering us timeless and out of the communication loop. Just one person in each group of eight was allowed to hold a watch. They would be our timekeepers, a job that would be rotated every now and then. Clocks, which usually hung in each classroom at Police College, were also noticeable by their absence. Initially I wasn't sure what not knowing the time would prove; however, as the days wore on, I became frustrated at not knowing how fast or slow our day was advancing. It took away the ability to forecast what might lie ahead.

That night we also met our 'drill sergeant'. He was probably quite nice outside of the role he would be playing for the next three days, but within it, as I was soon to find out during the time I had the displeasure of knowing him, he was a complete wanker. In my head, I called him Mr Snarky.

Our introductory day didn't finish until close to midnight, and we were then given our timings: breakfast at 7 a.m. and be ready to go at 7.30. After breakfast the next morning and unseen by us at the time, one of the applicants was removed from the course. He had failed the written test the night before. I became very aware that my being on this course might be very temporary.

Our first exercise was to complete the PCT and Cooper's. The PCT was like the District one, where you ran about 400 metres, jumped under and over some obstacles and dragged a 70-kilo dummy, but the Cooper's was a 12-minute run test. It was a set-distance run you had to complete within 12 minutes, and took place around the lagoon at Police College – a bit different from the District RFL.

We had awful weather that morning, and due to the rain were unable to complete the PCT at Police College where it was usually held. We were instead shepherded into vans with our assigned instructors, and driven to the Westpac Stadium in Wellington. It was freezing. When it was my turn, I coughed and wheezed my way round, delivering one of the poorest 400-metre times I had ever done – but because I'd turned another year older two days previously, the time allowed for me to complete it had gone up (we older girls sometimes get a good deal). I think I now had a time margin of roughly three minutes to do it in – or, as the jokes went, three days. I nearly coughed up a lung afterward. I felt like crap, with having the flu and it being so cold, but whereas I would normally have called in sick and asked for a hottie and hot chicken broth, today I was getting no sympathy from anyone.

Next, we all travelled back to College and ran our Cooper's. My time was good, despite my lumpy lungs, and after we finished we all sat under a tree refuelling and rehydrating in preparation for the rest of the three days. But – surprise, surprise – after we had sat back and watched the other section run the Cooper's, our section was told to get up and do it all again. *Bugger this*, I thought, but lined up with the rest. Away we went again. Let the mind-games begin.

We were then told to go to the swimming pool for the swim test. At District Selection I had had 10 blokes standing about while I self-consciously strode around in my togs; now I was contending with a course of 31, plus all the instructors. Through 'fiscal retentiveness', I had not purchased a new pair of togs to replace the creep-up-your-arse ones I had worn at District, but now, faced with this many onlookers, I wished I had.

With no knowledge of time, since I was alone in the girls' changing room with no watch, I got changed super-quick then sprinted up to the gym, frantically worrying that I was late. But aside from the instructors, who were all standing at the far end of the swimming pool, there was no one else from the course there. I ran up to the instructors, trying to look composed, then puffed out, 'Am I in the wrong place or first?'

'First,' said some straight-faced instructor. Then he added, 'Where's your rebar?'

My heart dropped, and I immediately turned and ran back the way I had come, without questioning him. There was no point in getting into a discussion about the fact we hadn't been told to take the rebar to the pool with us. By the time I reached the door, my arse cheeks were bare and my big black Speedo one-piece was now a thong.

Shit, shit, shit. I scurried down the stairs, grabbed the rebar and ran back upstairs. By the time I re-emerged, the whole course was lined up, in columns, facing my way. I ran toward them, noticing that no one else had their stupid bloody rebar with them. Just as I reached the group, the instructor who had sent me off stepped forward. 'You don't need your rebar,' he said.

Fucking good one, mate. I hope that at least for one second my face registered what I thought of him, but without saying anything I turned and ran back the way I had come. Holding the rebar in front of me in the same manner as you would carry a firearm managed to cause extra creepage of the best damn swimsuit in the world. I swore under my breath all the way back, hoping that by now the guys I was doing the course with were more concerned about passing the impending swim test than watching my undignified exit. No one ever said anything to me about it, so I imagine it was only ever a big deal in my world.

I returned without the bar, swam the swim, and put the experience down to character-building.

After the swim, we were given our first lot of scenarios. This was the main crux of the course. The physical component reveals certain character traits that you will display under pressure and tiredness, but the course is also designed to show how you perform your core role under pressure. It really does mimic what AOS life is actually like – rarely does the AOS pager go off when you've had eight hours of restful sleep. It's much more likely to go off on the night when you're only two hours into the much-needed catch-up sleep you had been promising yourself for the past two weeks.

I was given a Glock pistol with FX rounds, carried out my required safety checks and was given a set of instructions. 'Go through this door, turn right, engage the first target on the right, continue straight, then engage the second target on your left.' *Piece of wees*, I thought and away I went.

I walked in, turned right, walked a couple of metres, then saw my target – in this case, a cut-out baddie pinned to a wall. After shooting him twice, I kept walking straight ahead. I couldn't see the second target, but I soon came to a corner on my left. I crept toward it, slicing the corner like a pie until I was around it. Still no target. I walked all the way up to a barrier that was there, feeling a bit confused. It must have been a trap; there was no second target. 'End ex' was called, the signal that the exercise was over.

I holstered my weapon, followed the instructor back out, and was given the all-clear to proceed to my next waiting point. At a standard training scenario you would be given feedback, such as how well or how badly you did, and how you could improve next time. With this course there was no feedback at all. We were being watched, not taught. It gave you lots of opportunities to self-analyse, though, which was sometimes to your own detriment.

On the walk over to the next waiting area, I self-analysed the very brief scenario I had just done. There was only ever one target; that must have been it. When I arrived at the waiting area, however, I spoke to the guys who had gone before me. Each spoke of what they had done, and I found out that I had completely missed my second target. It had been placed on the wall prior to my turning left. I had been so focused on what was around the corner that I'd missed what was before it. *Great.* But fortunately, I found I wasn't the only one who had missed it. The result gave me a good learning experience, regardless of what the actual intent of it was – don't become so focused on a set of directions that you miss the actual goal.

The morning continued into the afternoon, with yet more scenarios and exercises to test our decision-making. Many of the scenarios were done wearing either safety goggles or FX masks – the latter look like Darth Vader type face-guards, and fog up after 30 seconds of exertion. They made everything look hazy due to the fogging, and became quite trying as the day wore on; but if you happened to get hit in the face with a stray round, they were worth their weight in gold.

Following the scenarios, we were sent up to the firearms range, lined up and put through our 'TOETs' (tests of elementary training skills). TOETs are also known as 'dry drills' – practising loading, firing and re-loading of firearms without using live ammo. After a long first day, the TOETs instructors became our first friendly faces. Although they didn't go overboard with enthusiasm and feedback, they weren't of quite the same ilk as our somewhat grim AOS instructors. They were probably breaking course rules by talking to us at all outside of telling us what to do, but I certainly wasn't going to tell them to shut up.

By now we'd had a couple of meals at the mess hall. All meals were bolted down without consideration of manners, who you were eating with, or polite small-talk. On previous College courses, I would take the time to hunt out a table with my fellow course-mates at it. This time around, I didn't care if I was next to the cook, recruits or high-ranking inspectors. There was food to be eaten, and there was always the possibility we could be called away part-way through.

We were watched all the time in the mess hall by Drill Sergeant Major Mr Snarky. He had already warned us that we would line up like everyone else, even though we would only have a matter of minutes in which to eat. On entering the mess hall, my heart would sink when I saw a line of recruits in front of us winding out the door and down the hallway. Sometimes they would helpfully wave us forward in the queue – they generally had a leisurely hour for eating lunch so didn't have the same time restraints that we did – but a glance back at Sergeant Major Snarky would have us wave off their offers with a firm but polite, 'No thanks.'

When eight of your 10 allotted minutes is spent in a line, it makes you a bit concerned about whether you'll be eating at all. When I arrived at the servery, I'd choose foods that were high in energy, required minimum chewing, and weren't likely to be vomited up if I had to run straight after I'd eaten. Taste was optional. Gobbling down food without a care for appearances became our new best operating procedure.

NATIONAL SELECTION

As well as the running tests we had to pass, and the running between scenarios that we had to do, we were also wearing full AOS kit for the entire day. Not being used to it, I was tired from the extra weight and found that it rubbed against collar-bones, hip bones, in fact most bones that weren't positioned about a centimetre from our internal organs. With the salt from sweat added to the mix, I was smarting all over.

That first day continued into the night, and at midnight (I'm guessing it was midnight), I found myself taking part in impromptu speeches. The first two minutes were spent talking about ourselves and the second two about a topic drawn from a hat. This was, again, a pressure scenario – taking you out of your comfort zone with the risk of blustering and bumbling in front of a group of people and making you as uncomfortable as hell. In my first 30 seconds I did a fleeting synopsis of my life, then proceeded to regale everyone with stories about my husband. He would have stuffed something in my mouth to shut me up if he'd been there, but he wasn't.

I mentioned him as being the skinniest man in the world, and how when he left the police section he used to work in they presented him with a pink detachable bottom made of papier mâché, as they all maintained he didn't have one. I talked about how every time I went away from home for any length of time and left him behind, he dispatched one or more of the animals on our 15-acre block of land. Either it was a home kill that needed to be done (this task completed 11 times), a particularly horrible domestic pet that had peed inside once too often (this task completed once), a squeamish neighbour having to get rid of a pet pig that had eaten one too many of something else (once), or the magpies that seem to kill every native bird that flies within 6 metres of our house (countless).

Then I got to my impromptu topic: 'Something, something, something Super 14, something, something'. I think the somethings that I can't remember had to do with names of rugby players, and I wasn't even sure 'Super 14' was rugby (I sought audience clarification on this), so the whole topic was a bit lost on me. I was jealous of the guy who had gone before me. His topic was 'Did Paris Hilton deserve to go to jail?' I could have *nailed* that one, but he didn't even know who Paris Hilton was! What a moron!

My lack of knowledge about New Zealand's national sport was something I was surprised hadn't been uncovered before, to keep me out of the AOS on that basis alone. I had tried countless times to enjoy it, but always found that I felt guilty sitting down watching TV for that long, especially as the first 20 times I would have to do it would be in order to acquire a taste for it. It wasn't exactly like that first cup of coffee you try as a teenager — a few minutes and it's all over. This was *two hours*. And I never could acquire the taste for it. I'm very sorry, New Zealand. I have tried.

So, for my given topic about which I had absolutely no knowledge, I decided to improvise. I talked about hating Sky Television because my husband's life revolved around it whenever rugby or cricket was on; that I didn't 'get' the game; then I moved back on to the subject of my husband killing things. I was gratified to hear a couple of titters and even saw a few smiles — all at my husband's expense. After two minutes I gratefully returned to my seat. I hoped that not being a rugby-head wasn't going to mean my demise on this male-dominated course.

At about two in the morning (so the section time-keeper told me), we were finally allowed to go. The watchkeeper's task was to wake everyone up for our next timing. The annoying facet of this for that person was that our sections had all been split up around the accommodation blocks at College. So the ones we shared a floor with weren't necessarily in our section. One section even had one member staying on a floor with a whole bunch of recruits, across the other side of the accommodation block. The splitting-up was a deliberate act, but I wasn't sure what it would achieve other than grumpiness from us.

Day one having ended in the early hours of the morning, day two seemed to start a matter of minutes after our heads hit the pillow. The poor assigned Wee Willie Winkies in reverse ran around the accommodation blocks hammering on everyone's doors at the assigned hour. At a quarter to five in the morning, having had about two hours' sleep, we were all lined up on the parade ground, wearing our blacks, with the army backpacks we were required to carry with us everywhere on our backs along with our body armour. Although the timing was given as 5 a.m., early on we had been warned that we always had to be wherever we were told to be 15 minutes beforehand.

After checking each other's kit out for neatness, presentation and, most importantly, presence – never leave something behind – we stood motionless in the darkness on the parade area. If someone had happened to walk around the corner at that time, they would have had heart failure, I think. They would have walked smack-bang into 31 black-clad, tired, but completely silent individuals, without having any warning of our presence.

While standing there, through my peripheral vision I could make out our Mr Snarky slinking around in the shadows watching us. Like soldiers, we stood ramrod straight, our rebars held in our hands, angled to face down to the ground on our left side. The big point was that we should all look the same; no one there fancied antagonising Mr Snarky by standing out.

Sergeant Major Snarky materialised out of the shadows at 5 a.m. on the dot – I presume it was that time as I had no watch and I'm sure we would have heard about it if we'd been late. He walked silently among us, stopping to eyeball an unfortunate member here, or to grab a strap which poked out 3 mm more than the next person's there. He would grab the offensive strap, tug at it and ask, 'What the fuck is this? Fix it up,' then would glower at the person standing in the line of sight of the strap, and give them a rip for not bringing it to the member's attention. 'You're a team. Start fucking acting like one!'

We were double-timed (running in lines two abreast) around for a bit, trying not to trip over each other or our rebars in the dark.

We arrived outside the gym and were sent inside to get into our running gear. Yay. More running.

This time, I couldn't be faffed running the long way round to the girls' changing rooms, so took the first of many shortcuts through the blokes' changing area. I encountered my first hassle when trying to get out the other side. All the doors and walls looked the same; I felt like a rat in a maze. I ended up in the urinal, then nearly in one of the toilets. Laughter and a small amount of guidance followed me as I finally found my way through to the other side.

PT next, with the pole. The combination of these two struck terror into my heart. The pole I remembered from my recruit days, all those years before. It was a power pole, and today we had to get in our sections and do a PT session with it. On my police recruit course we'd had to carry one of these around a 10-kilometre cross-country course, and shortly after I joined the police, OSH (Occupational Safety and Health) had decided to remove it from Police College training because it was deemed a hazard. I was thrilled to see that it had been reintroduced especially for our AOS selection course.

It was awful. I was the shortest by a long way, and a lot of the pole tasks involved holding it suspended above my head. For the taller guys in the group, i.e. everyone except me, it rested on their shoulders. If I was to be making any type of contribution at all, I had to hold it suspended above my shoulders, so it was all shoulder and arm work. And while I had worked hard on building up my shoulders bigger than they had ever been before, they were still those of a girl.

I was most surprised that I didn't knock myself out given the number of times I dropped the pole on my head as I slipped under it to give one shoulder a break in favour of the other. I swore at it to try to make it move. I swore at my parents for making me short. I swore at myself for wanting to do this. The guys swore at me for not lifting it higher – well, they didn't actually swear, just encouraged me on through gritted teeth. Throughout all this swearing and teeth-gritting, the pole mocked me. 'Bet you wish you hadn't come . . . why don't you go home? Just say the word and they'll let you go . . . just drop me, you know you want to!'

I was trying to do shoulder presses with it in an effort to keep it above my head, and knew that the others on my pole were finding their task even more difficult with me bumping and jumping about and ducking back and forth. Despite using as much 'intestinal fortitude' as I could summon, I wasn't able to hold the pole any higher. To cap it off, I saw that several other pole groups had five people in them, and we had four.

That morning's PT session with the pole was the closest I had ever come to quitting something. I don't think writing about it can do justice to how foul it really was. Perhaps it was made harder because of the lack of sleep; perhaps it was because of my previous bad relationship with the pole. Maybe it was because this was truly the most physically challenging thing I had ever done, and its challenge was coupled with the possibility of letting people down because of not being physically able to do it – regardless of how hard I tried. Whatever it was, it was a morning that no amount of money would ever make me repeat in my life. *Ever*. I hated that pole.

Throughout this session we were watched like hawks, told to speed up, slow down and, slowly but surely, worn down. At the end of this session, one guy quit. Just like that. So then there were 30.

When we were allowed to shower, this was done within a strictly limited time-frame. I love showers; they're my thinking time. Now my thinking time was removed completely. Soap was a briefly introduced accessory, and in the end seemed like a waste of time. Lathering it took up precious seconds I didn't have. But at least I had a new skill to add to my arsenal – fast showerer. Being on rainwater at home, this was a useful skill to hold on to, but I knew it wouldn't last past College. (It didn't.)

Another problem I encountered in the showers is one which perhaps only females understand – when trying to dress or undress quickly while being still slightly damp, the sports bras that pull over your head are a two-man operation. As you try to pull them down they roll up like a sausage skin on a cooked sausage, with your bits and bobs hanging out above and below the roll of sausage skin. For these pieces of fitness apparel to do their job (i.e. stop your wobbly bits wobbling too much) they have to be tight, and the combination of exhaustion and tiredness made achieving this almost beyond my capabilities. I couldn't hold my arms over my head to wrestle the bra over them because they were knackered from the pole-a-thon, so I got stuck, time and time again. During one such underwear battle on one of the selection course days, I enlisted the help of a recruit who happened to be in the locker room at the same time as me – a random woman who was at Police College learning how to be a police officer. I wanted to keep her with me for the rest of the course. She would have been The Bra Lady.

After the morning's pole exercise and breakfast, we were sent off to do team-building exercises. I treated this like the physical break it was. Apart from running from exercise to exercise, we could actually have a rest. I didn't do that well to begin with. The answers about how to cross crocodile-infested lakes with a toothbrush didn't come to me in a flash of lightning this time. The groups were continually mixed up during this exercise, so that the staff could see how each of us operated in different groups.

Because of the changing groups, I had to repeat one exercise. Recognising me as having already done it, the instructor told me to shut up and not give advice to the ones who were doing it now. I struggled with the shutting-up bit. I'm a bit of a talker. I tried to do sign language to the guys from behind a tree, to show them that the swing bridge idea they were using was crap, but I couldn't figure out 'crap' in sign language. My thumbs-down motion was read as, 'Oh – we should bring the bridge lower?'

In a few other exercises, like on the District Selection course, I had moments of clarity and problem-solved my arse off. Here was something I could finally do well on. The team and I dragged drums without touching them out of giant squares, armed only with two ropes; belly-crawled across shark-infested paddocks using four drums and a plank to save us from certain death; and balanced precariously on ammo containers to get from A to B without touching the toxic waste beneath.

Then it was on to more scenarios. Now that we were more tired than the previous day, our decision-making was even more closely scrutinised. One scenario that I vividly recall I will refer to as the 'corridor of death'. We were taken by van out to a large abandoned building in the Wellington area. Outside a set of swinging doors, we were each handed an FX face-mask, a loaded Glock, and one extra magazine with an unknown number of rounds in it. We weren't allowed to check how many rounds we had loaded, which was a clue that things were going to go pear-shaped. Our instructions were that on entering through the set of doors, we had to just deal with whatever presented itself.

With no idea about what 'whatever' was likely to be, I entered. The first thing I saw, directly in front of me, was a corridor leading forward to a seemingly empty room with its door open. Just before this room was another corridor leading to the right and out of sight. More immediately, however, to my hard left was a large counter – chest height – with a man behind it wearing an FX face-mask. Directly behind this man were two instructors wearing face-masks and fluoro vests, standing on a raised area behind the role-player with their backs against the wall.

The fleeting thought that dashed into my head was that the two instructors looked like they were hanging. From ropes. From the ceiling. Isn't that weird? Like from ropes, from the ceiling? What a strange thought process. I blame this on tiredness.

I took all of this in in a fraction of a second, during which time the man behind the counter approached, jabbering on about why he was there. I launched in with questioning as to why he *really* was there (with a quick, concerned look over his shoulder at the hanging instructors – shouldn't someone cut them down?). The story he gave was that he was a security guard, but he'd lost his job, blah blah blah. His rambling explanation led to the deduction that he was there unlawfully – for which I was to arrest and deal with him.

All the time he was blathering to me he was also advancing on me, repeating that he was allowed to be there. Now, when you have a Glock in your holster and are on an AOS course, you have the automatic presumption that your scenario will involve the use of it. With this so-called security guy, though, it was clear I wasn't going to be justified in shooting him just because he was in a building unlawfully. He had no firearm that I could see, and his hands were empty.

I warned him to stop advancing on me, which he didn't; so, fearing for my personal safety, I drew my training OC spray and pointed it at him. The training OC is just an inert water spray, which was there as one of our options for the use of force, and with which we had been issued at the beginning of the course.

As I pointed it at him I again warned him to stop, and told him if he didn't I would spray him. He kept coming, so I directed a squirt into his eyes. Except my squirt was more of a squir-r- . . . I had been given an all-but-empty canister; when I depressed the nozzle, a tiny bit of water leaked out of the end. The role-player looked at my scary squirter, then at me, and said, 'What's that supposed to be?'

'Beats me,' I said, and tried another squirt. Nothing at all came out this time. He kept approaching me, so I reached for the next weapon in my arsenal. My baton. As I reached for it, however, I think one of the instructors behind me must have been waving his arms frantically at the role-player, telling him to get down on the ground. The role-player's face-mask wasn't going to stop my tired and grumpy 50-something kilos of fury launching itself at him with my baton, which – unlike training OC spray – wasn't water-based.

Without my having to actually produce the baton, the role-player suddenly dropped to the floor with arms spread, saying, 'All right! All right! I'll get down!' I was just about to handcuff him when I was told, 'Move!', so, standing up, I turned back to the corridor to move to my next 'whatever', leaving the security guard face-down on the floor.

My next 'whatever' appeared faster than my reaction time. He popped into view in the room in front of me that had seemed empty, firing at me with FX rounds. I drew my Glock, screaming at him to put his gun down, and started firing back, but – not terribly surprisingly – I had been set up with a stoppage: a deliberately placed 'failure' round in my firearm that was designed to not work properly no matter how often I pulled the trigger. 'Stoppage!' I yelled out to no one in particular as I looked for cover. There was none, so instead I dropped to one knee and fumbled for a refill magazine, all the while getting nailed with hard, nasty wee FX rounds. They sting when they hit, and in my experience most role-players aim for any unprotected areas on the applicants. Usually the groin.

I finally got the new mag on, shot the baddie then advanced on his inert form. 'Can you hear me? Can you hear me?' I repeated as I advanced into the room. I kicked the gun away from him and stood over him trying to get a response. I had just begun to reholster my Glock and start first aid when again I was told, 'Move!'

I moved out of the room, and turned left down the corridor. A guy immediately popped out of a room in front of me, screaming at me, and I saw a glint of steel swing around in his right hand as he swung to face me. I challenged, drew and fired once at him, and straight away he fell to the ground. His weapon, which he was still holding in his right hand, clattered to the ground with him. 'You shot me! You shot me!' he yelled at me (which I took as a good sign – he was still alive).

'Stay on the ground! Stay where you are!' I yelled at him continuously as I advanced, my gun still trained on him. When I got closer, I kicked his weapon away. 'Why did you shoot me? Why did you shoot me?' he asked; then he stopped asking anything and gave a very dramatic death shudder, worthy of Shakespeare. Again

I sought a response from him with a view to carrying out first aid.

Moments later, ahead of me in the corridor another door swung open and a guy burst through, striding quickly and purposefully toward me. He started into his script straight away. 'What's happening out here? I've just been hunting and heard a noise!' He then looked at the guy on the ground, and started yelling at me. 'You've shot him! Why did you shoot him?'

I saw that he was holding a knife in front of him, and rear-slung over his shoulder was a rifle. While he was firing questions at me, he was also walking toward me with the knife. 'Put the knife down, put the knife down!' I started screaming, but he kept advancing, still holding the knife out toward me and challenging me as to why I had shot his mate.

When he got too close to me for me to protect myself, was still presenting his knife at me and still wasn't listening to my demands, I shot him. 'End ex.'

I holstered my weapon and looked back at the carnage down the hallway. The role-players were all climbing to their feet and dusting themselves off. What a hideous exercise. Every activity had been done at speed. It was probably all over in three minutes, but I could have sworn it took an hour. I was told to follow an instructor into another room, and after peeling off my sweat-filled face-mask I was interrogated about my reasons for use of force on each role-player. They were all justified under self-defence, but when I gave my answers they were in barely audible croaks – I had shouted so much as I'd challenged each role-player that I had nearly lost my voice. With the instructor barely acknowledging my answers and without any indication of whether they were wrong or right, I was sent into a holding area with the others who had already gone through. The corridor of death was over for me.

Subsequently, after every live AOS deployment I find that my throat is sore for the next four or so hours, either from yelling at house occupants to do or not do something or from carrying out clearance drills. To assist you in understanding the soreness, I would liken it to after a big night on the juice at a loud bar. You've spent the entire night yelling to be heard above the music or singing loudly to old ABBA songs, and by the time you head home you're only just able to squeak out your address to the taxi driver.

That evening following the corridor-of-death experience, we were bundled into vans again just as I thought it might be nice to get a rest. As we settled into our seats, we were given essay topics to do on the way to wherever we were going. The topic was 'Monarchy versus democracy'.

I get horribly car-sick. In fact, I also get train-sick, plane-sick, sea-sick, and any other movement-sick you can think of. I once made myself sick while I was driving. It was on a winding road. At the time I had a driving instructor next to me and I was trying to get a gold police driving certificate so that I could legally partake in high-speed pursuits. I knew, though, that any pursuit I would ever take part in would have to involve a straightish road – otherwise I would have to abandon it due to not being able to see the fleeing driver through the chunks of spew on the inside of the windscreen . . . But I digress.

So, writing my essay by torchlight in the back of a moving van was not pleasant. I started working on a serious debate on my true thoughts about the essay topic. Then I thought, *Bugger this. They're probably not even going to read it.* So I started to write about corgis. The queen has corgis, and I don't like them because I was once bitten by one. On the bum. I based the rest of my essay on that being my reason why we shouldn't have a monarchy. Not a very well-thought-out debate, I would have to say. I also added intermittent notes saying that I was going to have a break from writing as I was going to be sick. I would then place my pen down and gaze out the window at the darkness flying by, breathing deeply and thinking non-queasy thoughts.

Thankfully, after perhaps 40 minutes of driving – I'm guessing because it looked like they'd hidden the clock in the van's dashboard – we stopped. I gratefully leapt out and sucked in great lungfuls of seaside air. We were now on some far-reaching beach area on the south coast of the North Island, opposite to Wellington city. It was blowing a gale, and the brisk breeze made me shudder; partly from cold, but mostly from whatever we would next be embarking on.

Our orders were then received. We were told to line up in front of a whole row of jerrycans. These are water or fuel containers that I'd only ever seen armies use when carrying out deployments. Today, instead of leaving them to the army, we were assigned one jerrycan each, plus one extra to share around the group. We had on our body armour, too. I could tell this was going to be fun.

In unison, we stepped forward and picked up our jerrycans. I slung mine up on my shoulder, knowing that a hand grip wasn't going to last very long. We were briefed that for the entire walk, no jerrycan was allowed to touch the ground except, momentarily, during changeovers of the extra one. They weighed 25 kilos, and as soon as mine was on my shoulder I was keen to get going. The sooner we started, the sooner we stopped and the sooner I could put it down. One of the guys in my group picked up the extra can as well, and on 'Go!', our section set off at an orderly march, along with the other three sections.

Our walk was to take us along the coast, for goodness knows how far to goodness knows where. We were in a section of, I think, six at that time, and had an instructor following us. He was to give us no guidance or support, but was to monitor and assess us as we went. He would watch us for bitching, for slacking, or for putting down our jerrycans. There would be no alone time.

It was hard to say how far or for how long we walked with those jerrycans. I think it was about four hours; not quite an SAS 20-hour experience, but as I walked I found to my disbelief that it was strangely rewarding. I felt myself becoming all manner of clichés – thankful to be alive, thankful for this incredibly personal experience, thankful that I had worn the underpants that didn't go up my bum, thankful that my district had thought me worthy enough to send me on this selection course. It was extremely inspiring and memorable, and not at all what I had expected. I can't describe why I found it this way, as many people before me had talked of doing it and said it was really hard. They also told me how many people dropped out. Because I wasn't struggling with this like I'd originally thought I might, it gave me tremendous strength. If I could get through the really hard stuff like this, anything was possible.

Bearing the weight of one, and sometimes two, jerrycans, as the second can rotated around our section of six, I mostly became lost in my own thoughts; then the occasional look around would reveal a spectacular sight: the lights of Wellington on this clear night, reflecting off the stretch of harbour water that separated us from the city. Three times as we walked, I watched in awe as a large, silent mass drifted past on the water – the Wellington ferries doing their run. The fresh and blustery, salty sea air whipping around us seemed at that moment to be the cleanest air in the world, completing the *see, feel and taste* experience. You couldn't pay money for this.

When I felt that things were getting to a tiring point and my morale was slipping, I lost myself in my imagination. Despite enjoying what I was doing it was still incredibly hard work, so the dreaming was an excellent escape. I visualised myself in an already-booked two-night stay in a nice motel in central Wellington that my in-laws were shouting after I had finished the course. I pictured the spa bath, the dinner out, and the soft, warm bed. I would then hit a pothole in the dark, upset a blister that was rubbing and be jolted back to reality.

If a blister or an aching muscle began to become unbearably uncomfortable, I would tell myself that it was fine and I felt great. I was astounded when this mind-over-matter attempt actually worked! Aching arms from the two jerrycans diminished into *no problem* because I said it was so. Instead, I would concentrate on another part of me that felt fine. My eyeballs. They were relatively unscathed from the previous day's efforts, and they felt fine.

'Goodness me, my eyeballs feel great,' I would tell myself. 'Great, great, great. I have great eyeballs. They will take me far. I am very fortunate . . .' If the course instructors had heard about me thinking I was seeing staff hanging at a scenario, and learnt that I was now talking to my eyeballs while walking, I would be out. But they were my inner thoughts at that time, so no one was any the wiser.

All around me, all that could be heard was the gale that was whipping around us whenever we rounded an east-facing corner, as well as my team-mates' laboured breathing (combined with my own, of course).

During the walk we would constantly rotate leadership. The role of the leader was limited to trying to keep morale up, which was a hard task when no one was in a very high-spirited mood. One of the guys in my section in particular was extremely grumpy. His bad mood kept a smile on my face, though, as the grumpier he got the funnier he was. I dare say he didn't think he was very funny. I offered to tell him a grubby joke when he felt he was at his lowest point and that he should let me know when he reached it, but he was so focused on his own foul mood that he refused to take me up on it. He was, truly, wallowing in self-pity; and in a strange way, the lower he seemed to sink the stronger I felt. If a big, strong bloke struggled, by jingo, I would be finishing.

I got myself in a good routine with the jerrycan. I would carry it on one shoulder, then when that tired, would swap to the other. When I had both cans, I would carry one on one shoulder and the other in the opposite hand, then would take 50 steps. I would call that I was putting it down in five, four, three, two, one; then, on 'one', would put it down beside me and step to one side, allowing the next person behind me to pick it up. I would fall to the back of the line, then go through it all again, working my way to the front of the line and that second jerrycan.

In our team we'd decided how many steps we would be taking before moving the second jerrycan along, and 50 was the choice for some time. When the going got tough, a decision was made to reduce it to 35. I felt okay so kept it at 50, but made a point of counting my steps out loud as I walked. The instructor could hear from where he walked, so it had the extra effect of 'Look at me, I'm doing 50.' (About 30 minutes from the end, I noticed that a couple of the guys were counting only every right step, meaning they were in effect walking 100 — whoops: 'Don't look at me, 'cause I'm cheating.')

After turning around at perhaps the two-hour mark, we trudged back, getting whipped around by the wind all the way. The home straight. Looking back, although I wouldn't put my hand up for it again, the jerrycan walk was an experience that I will always remember. I think this is because if I was told to do it off my own bat, I would never have thought I could have achieved it.

The mind-games continued when the walk was nearing its end. Seeing the vans, some of the guys called out encouragement to those in our group who were struggling, saying we were nearly there, and that sort of thing. I cut in with a reminder that it might not be the end, and to be prepared to keep going. And on cue, we were made to walk right past the vans.

When we were finally allowed to part with our jerrycans, we all lined up at a fence and stretched against it. We were shattered. Some blisters are hard to feel when you move — they just feel like a hot spot — but as soon as you stop, you are very aware of them. As we all peeled ourselves off the fence to get into the vans for the ride back (or what we hoped was the ride back), every one of us was limping to some degree. I didn't know — and still don't know — how far we walked, but it was a long time on the feet.

Our walk took us to perhaps about midnight. Of the four sections, we lost two or three applicants through injury on the jerrycan walk. I think one of the injuries was a back strain and another may have been a rolled ankle. One of the injured members was my team-mate from Palmy with whom I had travelled down. When I learnt he was gone, I felt gutted. We had already been through a lot together in District Selection, and to have got to this point and no further,

I knew he would be absolutely devastated. It also meant that from the original three of us from Palmerston North who had passed selection, we were now down to two.

We climbed back into our respective vans, a lot quieter than when we started, and were told to keep going with our essays. I was soaked with sweat from the walk and, like the others, sucked back as much water as I could. I then set to finish my literary masterpiece on the Queen and her canines. On the way, though, with all the water drunk and the physical exhaustion, I had to give a frantic tap on a team-mate's shoulder and he told the driver to stop. I leapt out and threw up in a bush on the side of the road, on the Wellington motorway. Lovely stuff.

Back at Police College, we were told to sort all our kit out – the body armour we had worn on the walk was pretty sweat-drenched by now, and our boots could surely do with a shine. Wondering if bed was getting any closer, we were then told to sit at our desks again. It wasn't quite bedtime yet.

We had to watch a video of a vehicle driving around – with the view being from inside the vehicle. We weren't told what to look for, but as the video played, it would stop for a second and a question would be asked, such as, 'What was the last street name you passed?' or, 'What colour was the car that was pulling out on your left?'

Simultaneously, we had a map to follow the route of the car on. The next question would be, 'Where are you now?' As I had been lost for the preceding five minutes of video, my logical answer was, 'No bloody idea.'

We were also pulled out of the class one by one and given an observation test, which wasn't as bad as the video, and had to demonstrate one of the knots we'd been taught. In fact, every now and then during our course we were pulled away from our section and asked to demonstrate one of these infernal knots. They were a 'down time' exercise we had to perform. I had an odd way of doing a few of them, and could see that the instructor was confused just watching me. Miraculously, they still came out okay.

The previous day I had had an anxious moment when I thought I had lost my rope. I usually left it in a side pocket of my pack, but seeing that people were getting pulled away one by one to show off a knot, I had gone to get mine to prepare – but couldn't find it. I was cringing at what was going to happen when they learnt I had lost something; I was going to get roasted alive! But I sure as hell wasn't going to tell them if I could help it.

After the most recent knot-tyer had walked away from the instructor, I sidled up to him and asked if I could borrow his rope. He handed it over on the sly, and when I was next called up I used it in lieu of my lost one. That wasn't going to solve the problem of where the hell mine was, though. After completing my demo, I returned the rope to its owner and went back to my pack to have a decent search. I immediately found what the problem was. It wasn't my pack I'd been looking in. I finally located mine, which – funnily enough – looked exactly the same as the other 29 laid out on the ground.

The observation tests finally ended at about 2 a.m. and we were allowed to head off to bed. But, before we left, we were told to be prepared for a call-out. This was something they hung over our heads on both of the two nights' 'sleep' we had – that we might get called out. We never did, thank goodness. And we had now finished day two.

Moments later (or perhaps a couple of hours), we were woken. This was our final day. As soon as I got out of bed, I nearly cried out aloud. Blisters. Throughout all the training I have ever done, I have never managed *not* to get blisters. I think I must just be one of those people predisposed to them.

We all lined up on the parade area 15 minutes prior to the chosen hour – 5 a.m. again. Mr Snarky was slinking around the shadows waiting for us all to form up, as he had done the previous morning. However, as he walked through our ranks this time, he had a particularly happy moment when he discovered someone had forgotten his numbered bib. The glee he showed on his face was the type of glee one wanted to punch out. The member concerned recounts his memories of this fatal moment. Of wanting the ground to open up and swallow him. Of wishing it were someone else who had forgotten their number seven bib, and not him.

The concerning thing for us, though, was the delight Mr Snarky took in keeping surprisingly quiet about his discovery. We thought he would have yelled, called us all rude names and made us do press-ups until our arms fell off – like he had been doing for all manner of tiny misdemeanours previously. Instead, we did perhaps only 20 press-ups – which the poor bib-less one was made to watch – then he left him with the menacing words, 'I'll sort out something for you later.'

We were sent into the gym changing rooms, then up into the gym. In twos we were put through an upper-body circuit. I worked out the trick for this. Let your face register as much pain as you can, and hopefully you'll look convincing in your effort. After a bit, my face just did its own thing anyway – grimacing and contorting with all the things I was feeling. I recall once reading some ridiculous bit of advice in a fitness magazine: when weight-training, relax your face as it uses lots of energy in your facial muscles to grimace. What a crock. Try to do the most extreme exercise you can think of with a relaxed face. It doesn't work like that. My partner for this was Mr Grumpy from the jerrycan carry. He seemed to have recovered from the previous night's torture and was motivational to me – which was good, because I needed it. I was spent.

Mr Bib-less's punishment arrived after this session. For forgetting his bib, he was introduced to a new rebar. This one weighed about 25 kilos, and had to be carried everywhere like his previous 5-kilo one. His love for our instructor went up a notch that morning, as he had to jog wearing body armour, carrying his backpack, and now with an added 20 kilos of punishment.

After speedy showers and speedier eating, we had more scenarios like the corridor of death. Again, now that we'd had two days with minimal sleep, our reactions and justifications were even more rigorously tested. I averaged about three good scenarios and one humdinger crap one.

Straight after lunch, we went through a stress shoot. This involved wearing a gas mask, running to get the heart rate up, and then shooting designated targets. My biggest hassle was not being able to see through a fogged-up mask after my run, but I wasn't alone in this. After finishing up here, we were seen to by medics, told to empty our packs, and given our final assignment.

Through all that we had achieved thus far, there was one exercise that hadn't yet cropped up. The Battle Efficiency Test. This was the requirement to walk 12 kilometres in under 1 hour 50 minutes, carrying 25-kilo packs. I hadn't had too much difficulty with it at District Selection, but we were now into the third day, my blisters were huge, and I was getting pretty tired.

Our time-keeper let us know when two o'clock rolled round, and we were marched down to the parade ground and directed to our empty army packs. Beside each one was a full jerrycan. We were given instructions to place this inside the pack, then were told the intended route. I approached the pack, did the jerrycan thing, and lifted it; it felt as if it weighed half a tonne. I was worried. Very worried. I slung it onto my shoulders, lined up with everyone else, and then we were off. I tried to make a sprightly start, but felt the straps biting in, my blisters rubbing and, worst of all, my morale ebbing away.

I concentrated on the ground in front of me, and nothing else. If I looked up, I could see others disappearing ahead of me, bouncing their packs on their shoulders as if they were feather-light. My pack was a little under half my body weight, and certainly felt anything but feather-light.

Within the first 20 minutes I had taken the first of my supplements, the same sticky liquid I'd taken at District that had stuck to my leg in a most annoying fashion. I was the one who had chosen this particular energy food so it was my fault, but I wanted to just chuck it away this time so it wouldn't gum up in my leg pocket again. In the end, my tidy Kiwi upbringing wouldn't allow me that moment of naughtiness.

I was near the back right from the get-go and, try as I might, couldn't go any faster. At one point I was even last, which I hated; but then, on the way back, I leant on the mantra I had used in training. I would not fail my district. I would not fail my colleagues who had supported me in my quest. I would not fail myself. But, most importantly, I would not fail my husband who believed I could do this.

I also visualised my five-year-old son standing on the side of the road encouraging me. In my mind he was on my husband's shoulders, waving a flag, and he was saying 'Come on, Mummy!' I laughed to myself at the madness of this imagery, but it did boost me. Failure to complete this wasn't just failing me, but failing my family. I gritted my teeth and, with a view of the other applicants grunting forward in front of me, began to jog one power pole, walk the next, jog one, walk one.

My pack was listing severely to the left, but this ended up being a good distraction away from the self-pity trap I was falling into, so I didn't try to fix it. *Run one, walk one; run one, walk one.* I passed a few guys, setting my sights up ahead. Then a couple of guys passed me back — who wants to be beaten by a girl? — then I passed them again. This went on a couple of times, until I felt I had no more in me. I was like a car running out of petrol. Then I thought I might *want* to run out of petrol. Did I really need to finish? I again kicked myself. *Yes, I would finish.*

Then I remembered the supplements, and downed two more. Gut-wrenching cramps were rather immediate as I hadn't taken enough water with them, but they did give me a much-needed push. And I didn't give a stuff about them sticking to me any more.

I rounded the last corner, and was faced with the small hill heading back into College. My breathing was now a loud noise as opposed to a gentle in and out of air, and I tried to raise the last bit of strength needed to jog up the hill and pass the guy in front.

Nope; I was on empty. I staggered over the line, someone helped me get the pack off, and my legs finally buckled. I was finished.

I stood up and staggered around for a little bit, completely overcome physically, mentally and, rather embarrassingly, emotionally. I felt tears pricking my eyes, and I sucked in great lungfuls of air to keep those impending tears at bay. I wobbled my way up to one of the guys on my section who had come in just behind me and doubled over beside him, slapping him on the back to give myself a focus other than wanting to blubber shamelessly. It seemed to provoke him, though – great wracking, heaving sobs came out of him, which made me feel much better. I had found my limit, and so, it appeared, had he!

I was then beckoned over to an instructor. *But wait, there's more!* Shit – I had forgotten there was more to the BET than just the pack walk. Standing next to the instructor was a nice, neatly dressed recruit. 'How much do you weigh, Williams?' I was asked by the instructor. *Williams? Not Number Five?* At least I wasn't a number any more.

'55 kg,' I said.

'How much do you weigh?' the instructor asked the recruit.

'65,' she answered. Close enough, they declared. I approached her purposefully, gave her instructions not to wriggle if she felt herself sliding, then hoisted her onto my shoulder. Crikey! 65 kg my arse! What sort of time was this for a woman to lie about her weight?

With the lying woman now causing me to stagger around under her weight, I was given a cone as a turnaround point and wobbled off toward it. I felt her slipping, and told her to stay still. The poor thing was getting my horribly sweaty shoulder rubbed into her navel, which must have been particularly unpleasant; but as long as she didn't move, we would get along just fine.

As I neared the end cone, I felt myself slow down, then falter. I heard people yelling encouragement and, with eyes glued to the cone, I literally staggered to it. The silly thing is that if you want to get to a particular point, you should always look beyond it. I mean this both metaphorically and literally. As I was only looking at the cone, my body was only going to take me as far as the cone and not a millimetre past it. At the last moment, I clicked to what I was doing and focused instead on the hurricane fence up past the cone. And as I stumbled past it, I was told I had made the 100 metres. Good enough for me.

I gratefully dropped the poor sweated-on girl to the ground, without any energy to thank her – and then was given my next task. *You've got to be bloody joking.* My rib was sore, I was absolutely fucked, and I had more to do?

I went in the direction they had pointed me in, which was the College gym. A long rope attached to the ceiling stared at me. One of my course-mates was busy clawing his way up it, but kept on slipping back down before he hit the top. He was clearly stuffed and had no strength left.

Luckily, I had done rope climbs before. It wasn't so much about strength, but about foot technique. When it was my turn, I shimmied up and shimmied down. *Done.* I then had to jump the 2-metre wall, which I did. I was viewing these tasks as stupid and annoying things that had to be done if I was going to be allowed to go and have a shower, which I was hanging out for.

The very last thing was a horizontal leap – a leap from one point to another laid out on the gym floor. *Done.* I was done. *Done, done, done. Fuck you very much for coming. Now let me go and lick my multiple wounds in peace.*

We were all gathered up, told the course had been completed, and allowed to go and get ready for a barbecue. *Yahoo!* We were free. Having just been pushed to, then beyond, my limit, I felt surprisingly alive and invigorated now that it was over. And here I had been thinking I would just collapse into a heap and start crying. As soon as I was handed my cellphone back I phoned my husband and told him I had survived, then trudged up the 10 flights of steps to the barrack room. My floor-mates and I all congratulated each other, ourselves, the Queen – anyone we felt deserved it – and flitted around the barrack room, not one of us now feeling the slightest bit tired. We had all conquered what was arguably one of the hardest courses the police held.

One of the guys I shared a floor with gave me an earnest and heartfelt slap on the back. He told me that when he'd first met me he'd thought I wasn't going to make it, but I had proved him wrong. Having peer praise and acknowledgement was the highest form of praise for me. I was chuffed with myself, and with all of these guys, for achieving what we had achieved. Each one of us had dealt with our own issues throughout – such as the guy who did the course with seven stitches in the palm of one hand and a 'bung' ankle. Another guy's blisters – in fact, the guy who had praised me – were the worst I had ever seen. He lost the skin on the entire underside of both feet, but still got through the BET.

The biggest hassle from then on was that we had stopped long enough to let the pain set in, which it certainly did – tenfold. After a gorgeous shower, we all limped our way down for our barbecue and much-deserved ale. I felt like I had been run over by a truck, I was that sore. I tried to imagine being asked to run again now, and felt there wasn't a snowball's hope in hell of that – but also knew that if the course had still been going on, we would all, somehow, manage to find that bit more in reserve.

At our barbecue, I sat opposite Mr Snarky. Although the hard stuff had finished, I was sure you could still be kicked off, so I, like the rest, was still reserved around the instructors. I knew that Mr Snarky had only been playing a role for the last three days, though, so I struck up a conversation with him. And what do you know? He *was* a nice guy. He knew some other words aside from the F word. He was interesting, and clearly very focused on making good AOS members. There was every chance he might one day have to work with any one of us on a job, so it was in his best interests to make sure he wasn't letting incompetent jack-arses through onto district squads. I forgave him over a beer.

That night brought a long but unsettled sleep. Every time I rolled over, I disturbed some dormant injury or blister. I had taken every painkiller I could get my hands on prior to hitting the hay, but it didn't make much difference.

The next morning, we all packed and said our farewells. It had only been three days, but I had got to know some of the guys quite well in that time. I was looking forward to meeting them again in less taxing circumstances. We had a profound new respect for each other, knowing what we all had gone through.

But I had one more physical feat that I looked set to fail on: I couldn't carry my bags downstairs. I heaved and groaned with the sheer weight of them, letting both fall down the steps. The motion of pulling caused indescribable pain in my ribs, and in the end, in frustration, I had to enlist the help of a female police officer who was also from Palmy and down at College on another, less physical course!

The next few weeks involved lots of recuperation. My soreness came from blisters, bruises and pulled muscles, but also a popped rib cartilage gained in one of the many physical exercises we had been through. I took a much-needed break from training, and tried to settle back into a 'normal' existence again – minus the frantic training schedule.

Then I got the word. While some people who had passed the course still did not get selected to attend qualifying, I had. *You beauty.* It was to be my final hurdle before getting into the AOS.

6

AOS QUALIFYING COURSE

Unlike the previous two courses, the qualifying course was there to teach you the trade – not to break you. My one regret regarding my selection was that the other Palmy candidate wasn't going through with me. There was only one spot for Palmerston North at the qualifying course, and I had got it due to my longer service. He was an awesome guy, both personally and operationally. He was, however, guaranteed the next spot the following year, which he did go on to fill.

I was looking forward to the qualifying course. There were quite a few weeks to go – it was set to start in August – and it was fair to say that I wasn't as fit as I had been. The date arrived sooner than expected. My husband had sorted his work hours to suit child-care in my absence, so with a tear in my eye and a vehicle packed to the roof with kit, I waved my little family goodbye.

I got a ride down with two guys I had been on National Selection with, both from the Hawke's Bay. Like on the previous course, we would need to know our use-of-force law verbatim and we also had a raft of other pre-course reading materials, so we used the two-hour travel opportunity to brush up on what we didn't know. On arrival, we checked in and once again I dragged my case up three flights of stairs to my new home for the next three weeks. And there, standing in the doorway, was an apparition. Another girl! Her name was GB (not her real name, but the one we've agreed to call her).

GB was a little taller than me, about the same weight and, as I found out as the course progressed, a great source of inspiration. At that time she was the only operational female dog handler in New Zealand, so she had already broken into one of the last male bastions in policing. I imagined that the AOS wasn't going to be too much of a drama for her.

We also found that we were the only two on our floor, which meant no queue for showers, no glimpses ('accidental' or otherwise) of partially naked blokes, and no foul-smelling lavatories at 7 a.m. As we made preliminary small-talk, we unpacked our assortment of chocolates, herbal teas, lollies and other items that we had deemed were necessary for survival over the next three weeks.

I think this may be one of the many differences between boys and girls. Boys worry about things when they crop up – i.e., at 10 p.m. on a Tuesday evening they might think they wouldn't mind some chips, but unfortunately they don't have any, so they just cope without. Girls, on the other hand, are absolutely prepared for food urges of whatever sort, at any given moment. Not only will they have the chips, but they will also have a selection of them as well as accompanying dips.

Boys getting ready to watch a game of rugby will have beer, and that's it. Stretched, they might have a bag of chips. Girls would have two large platters of nibbles containing such things as grapes with toothpicks through them, a selection of cheeses, and wine to go with each variety of cheese. They would also have either freshly laundered doilies or coasters on any table surface that might, during the course of the match, have an item placed on it. A word, then, to any blokes on a course, police or otherwise: if craving something at an odd hour or wanting a little bit more than just beer with your game, hunt down the nearest female. I guarantee she will have a supply of whatever food you need.

GB and I got on well immediately. I would almost go so far as to say we were like peas in a pod. Although we look completely different, we both have determination, tenacity and drive, and the stubbornness to overcome whatever is chucked in our way. As I talked to her, I saw a lot of me. She was a cut above, though – she had also achieved domination in a male-dominated field, that of the police dog handler. I had always thought I couldn't do that job because many police dogs weighed what I weighed and I stood a snowball's chance in hell of getting one over a fence. But here was GB. All that *and* a packet of chips.

Not only was she here to become an AOS member, but she was also required to train her dog to AOS standard on yet another course. After this present course, aside from yearly fitness testing, my AOS courses were done. Not so for GB. She was just beginning. Her dog Fang (also not his real name, but very appropriate), was kennelled up while his handler was subjected to the qualifying course.

That night, after unpacking and sorting ourselves out, we walked down to the classroom for the introductions and course opening. They also chucked in the written test that we had brushed up on during the trip down. I was happy I knew enough to pass; but while the selection course had been three days of pressure, I was now about to embark on three weeks of it. Despite the fact that it was a teaching course where the point was to learn about how to operate in an AOS capacity – and not just be deprived of sleep and pushed to our limits like the previous courses – it was still also pass or fail. True to form, one guy failed the written test and was kicked off that first night.

Later, we were allowed to return to our rooms. GB and I began what was to become a regular habit: a herbal tea, lollies, and a yak over a cuppa. Over the next few weeks, I found that on some of the particularly bad days I hung out for these informal debriefs. They kept me sane.

AOS QUALIFYING COURSE

The first week of the course was utterly fantastic. We would have a classroom lesson on a skill or drill, then be sent out to try it. We utilised local disused buildings and stormed through them, dressed from top to toe in black, feeling professional and extremely privileged to be allowed to do this role. As anyone finds when trying a new skill, although I had seen some of them practised they weren't anywhere near as simple or as easy as they looked. We went over them again and again and again, but I always hated it when the day was finished and we were loaded up into vans and taken back to College. I wanted to keep going. I found myself thinking that the only reason I was glad I hadn't been able to do this job earlier in my police career was that I probably wouldn't have wanted to stop long enough to have a child. I think I would have been too addicted.

After the first week (in which we did more than 85 hours of training), we had our first progress meetings with our assigned instructors. My instructor looked like Mr Incredible. He gave me an okay report, and I looked forward to what the next week would entail. GB was the same. We were in different sections, which was good – it gave us something to talk about at the end of the day over our sweet treat and cup of tea.

My section was an awesome bunch of people. A complete cross-section of individuals. I once spoke to a trainer about AOS members' personalities. He described them as mostly 'type A'. Imagine, then, a whole bunch of type As together – lots of loud chiefs with no Indians! Our group got on really well, though. There was The Joker, Mr Serious, Mr Grubby, Mr I'm So Laid-back I'd Like To Go To Sleep, Mr Quiet, the Sergeant Major, and me. When days were tough, we would slap each other on the back, give each other some morale-boosting advice, and then just get on with it.

I think our section's instructor, Mr Incredible, had a hard time not treating me like the girl I was. In week two, the pressure began to come on. While we had been taught the skills in week one, week two was all about applying them under pressure and under scrutiny; always under his watchful gaze. I began not to have such a fabulous time. When I stuffed something up, instead of just yelling at me like he did with the boys, Mr Incredible would pull me away from the group and, in the manner of a school teacher trying not to upset a five-year-old child, would explain to me what I had done wrong. His tone, though, was always, 'Now Liz, blah, blah, blah.' I began avoiding eye contact with him after each drill. If he looked at me, it might be followed with an expression that showed disappointment and the need for a subsequent lecture, then one-on-one instruction.

Unfortunately, I'd done one thing to put the spotlight on me in the beginning. We had been clearing (flushing out the baddies from) a large corridor that had dozens of rooms leading off it. Each room was cleared in a set fashion. To stop baddies learning our tricks of the trade, I'll leave the explanation of what we were doing at that. While doing this room-clearing on this particular day, one of the instructors poked his head out of a room that we were working our way toward. He was playing our bad guy for the day. When he poked his head out he had a big, silly grin on his face and was holding a foam mattress.

I got to the room and, as I was about to enter, he chucked the mattress at me – still wearing his goofy grin. I stepped out of the way of it, letting it fall to one side. We were supposed to be training seriously, but I let my guard down a bit at his grinning face.

I can't remember exactly what happened after that, but shortly afterward I was called to one side. *Uh oh.* 'We are a little concerned about what went on back there. You balked.' I did *what?* I had no idea what he was talking about. Blow by blow, he explained what I had done. *You mean hesitating because one of the instructors was grinning at me like a Cheshire cat as he threw something made of foam at me? You've got to be kidding! How am I meant to play my serious role with him looking at me like that?* But I wasn't about to enter into a debate about it. Grin or no grin, I still had a job I was meant to be doing. I said it wouldn't happen again. Apparently, however, it did. In the next scenario, I was told that I hesitated for a split-second before entering a room. I picked up my game, but was struggling under the pressure of knowing that now four sets of eyes were watching me on every room entry. I felt that the rest of the team might as well have not been there – I thought I was the only one getting scrutinised that day.

I watched a couple of the other sections do their room entries. No one was perfect, but as I had picked up the focus, I would have to do something pretty spectacular to get rid of it. Unfortunately, I didn't – I got remedials, a.k.a. retraining. I was devastated.

I was told after tea one night to meet the instructor down at the scene-of-crime house, but I wasn't told what for. The scene-of-crime house is a training set-up – a house at Police College that is inside a building. It is minus its roof and there is a walkway above it that you reach by going up a set of stairs. When carrying out any number of training opportunities at College, your classmates and instructors get to hover overhead and look down at you – a bird's eye view as you walk between the rooms.

After the arrangements had been made, the guys at my table all looked at me questioningly. I shrugged my shoulders nonchalantly. No big deal. But inside, I was crapping myself. What did I have to go there for? Was I going to get my marching orders? I went down 10 minutes early, and was the only one there. Oh god – they had pulled me away from the group to tell me the bad news: *Liz. Sorry but we're going to have to let you go. You're crap. Mr Incredible has been trying to help you, but all you do is mock his chin – don't deny it, we've heard you.* They'd probably then let me up to the barracks to pack while everyone else was busy doing something else. No one would even know I was gone. I thought about my return to district, having failed. I thought about quitting the job. Yes, I would quit. That was the only solution.

One of the instructors finally came in and sat down on a couch near mine. It was the Cheshire cat. He made polite conversation about the weather. *Who gives a shit about the weather?* 'Are you going to kick me off?' I finally asked him, close to tears.

'No, no. Nothing like that. We've just seen something that could be a problem in your room entries, and we're going to take you through it to help you.' I nearly cried in relief. But relief was short-lived. Remedials! What kind of person who is in training to become a lethal weapon gets friggin' *remedials*? Did 007 get remedials? Did that character Mel Gibson played in all those films get remedials? No! Of course they bloody didn't! I was pissed off. And deeply embarrassed.

Two other instructors turned up, one with a video camera. *Joy.* One of them became my 'wingman', and away I went, having every single one of my room entries filmed and analysed. After every entry where I encountered a bad guy – who would be throwing something at me as I entered – I would have the video 'evidence' played back and pulled apart. 'See what you're doing here?' I was asked.

'No,' I honestly said. They all crowded around the tiny screen and played it again. And again. And again. I couldn't see it at all. I was feeling that my perceived problem was increasing in magnitude in their eyes only.

'Perhaps it might be easier to see with a bigger screen,' one of them admitted. *Or perhaps I could shove the handicam up your arse and see how it plays widescreen out of your mouth?* By now I was coming very close to actually doing something bad with the video camera. At this point, with those evil thoughts in my mind, I did what they thought was a good, aggressive room entry. 'See this? This is good. What was different with this one?' I was asked.

I decided that honesty was the best policy. 'I was thinking, "Fuck you lot" when I came in,' I said. This was greeted with laughter, but from then on, that was indeed how I did all my room entries. Angrily and aggressively. Maybe I was a pacifist at heart, and this was unwittingly how I entered every time – like I wanted to sell flowers and goodwill and peace to all mankind, not dominate the room with my presence. Although being singled out for remedials sucked, it did teach me a good skill.

Nowadays, when going into a job I flip a switch. Nice Lizzy. Not-nice Lizzy. I could also liken the 'flip' to going from being a passive dog, like an old, partly blind Labrador that wants to be everyone's friend, to one of those insane, small terrier breeds that will do anything if you throw them a ball, and on this day just wants to get into someone's house so they can sprint in and rip them to bits in an effort to get that ball!

After 40 minutes of critiquing at my remedials, I was allowed to go. I again felt imminent tears pricking my eyes as I headed back up to the barracks. I was tired from our long days and nights, and although I had learned a valuable lesson, I had hated being singled out. And, right on cue, when I rang my husband to tell him what had happened, I burst into tears. The poor guy. As I blubbed out my day's misery, GB came in. I think she thought I had just got news that someone had died. When I got off the phone, I blubbed out to her what happened, and she said all the right things. We celebrated my breakdown with a cup of herbal tea and chocolate – and I blazed forward the next day as if the previous day's events had never happened. Perhaps the most heartening thing was that as the course evolved, I talked about what had happened with course-mates and found out that I wasn't the only one who'd been singled out for remedial treatment. At least, that's probably what they told me to make me feel better.

Then there was the day of the gas lesson. The gas used by the AOS is lovely stuff that makes your eyes stream and your nose clog up with snot, then allows the same snot to pour out of your nose (and quite possibly eyeballs) in relentless waves of mucus. It bites into your sinuses above your eyebrows and your forehead, and somehow even makes it to your ears. It doesn't differentiate between ladies and gentlemen, and it is all-invasive. Something to perhaps try at home to get an idea of what gas is like, is to get a significant other to stand in front of you while you are sitting in a chair. While eating about four teaspoonfuls of wasabi, get them to sprinkle pepper into your eyes and then smear the remaining wasabi up your nostrils. Then breathe deeply and think about defiance.

Our lesson this day began with four of us kitted out in gas masks and full AOS kit – the good guys; and the other half of the section wearing just overalls and nothing over their faces – the bad guys. A gas canister was set off near a small outdoor building, then the unprotected bad guys were made to run around it a few times and do some press-ups. The kitted-out ones acted as the safety team.

My time as a bad guy arrived. We hurled a bit of abuse at the other section members who were kitted up; then, when a gas canister was thrown at us, we ran around the back of the small building. Then we were told to start doing laps.

My second lap around the building after the gas had been let off was my demise. Gas works on pain. When it is breathed in through the nose and mouth, it hurts. When you breathe out, it hurts. Your eyes hurt when they are open. Your eyes hurt when they are closed. Your skin burns. When you breathe in and get a large lungful, you end up in a mild state of panic, so you try to breathe out, which increases your state of panic. Tenfold. Someone has taken away all your air. You start to hyperventilate. It takes away all thought of resistance and fight. You become a blithering, blubbering, dribbling mess. *I will go anywhere with you when I am in this state.* Except back to open up another gas canister.

After I had had lots of water poured over my head and face, I was faced round into the wind, and started to slowly regain my composure. I was then sent off to the next activity for the day. It involved sweating – which reactivated the gas I still had on my skin from the previous gas lesson, and proceeded to give me a secondary burn. Then, at the end of the day when I was allowed to have a shower, this activated the burning all over again. I fail to understand how bad people don't come out when this stuff is fired into their house. I will always come out, I promise you that.

On the Saturday of the second week of the course, we had an exercise that enlisted the help of a recruit course. It was a simulation of the Columbine High School shooting of 1999, with active shooters on the loose and the police recruits playing the role of the terrified students. Scattered somewhere among them were our active shooters. We were split into teams, given directions, and sent off to do our thing. The recruits had also been given a brief – how the instructors wanted them to react to us. The adrenaline on this exercise was high, and I could only imagine how much more stressful it would be if it were for real. Real offenders, real bullets, real students.

In my section, we were to clear a building, deal with any offenders, and locate and save hostages. We entered as per our practised drills, and early on I located a recruit who had a rather gruesome and realistic hand wound – his finger had been blown off. Using my limited skills as a medic – which I was not – I dressed it using the bandaging we were always required to carry, then prepared to keep moving. By now I could hear shooting from the room in front of me. While I was held up doing my nursey duties, I had missed all the action. I waited for them to make their way back to me; when they appeared I tacked my hostage on behind the three they had saved and we walked them out to a safe area. Mission one completed.

We returned to Zero Alpha (the command base for the exercise), and were given our next mission. Although it was a different building, our job was effectively the same. Enter, deal with offenders, save hostages and secure the building.

As we stealthily approached our target building, one offender popped up through an upstairs window, fired a shot in our general direction, then disappeared again. This let us know that we were dealing with at least one villain. We entered the building and cleared our way upstairs, not meeting any resistance on the way. So far, so good. Unfortunately, by the time we got to the room we had seen our person in, I was about fourth in line and therefore missed all the action yet again, my team engaging with fire from the front. One offender was taken out, but who knew how many more were left?

I was then one of two who entered this huge room, packed from floor to ceiling with books. They were everywhere. The location we were at was a disused high school, and it looked as if every book in the place had been stacked in this room when the school was closed down. As we entered, my team-mate and I called out our presence, waiting for someone to pop up, but all I could hear in response was my own heavy breathing.

The room-clearance work was really physical, especially so when it took up a full day and was spread over an entire high school. Over time, the full kit I wore became more comfortable and less cumbersome, but as this was only my second week of wearing it all, I was finding it hard going. Sweat was pouring off me, and as we were using FX, I had goggles on that fogged up as I heated up. I needed windscreen wipers inside them.

I advanced down to the end of the room; then, just when I thought I had cleared everywhere, I noticed that a bench against a wall had a line of books stacked right up to it. Crouching down, with Glock and eyes searching together, I looked behind it. Right at the very back was a hostage. Studies have shown that hostages will often hide from their rescuers. They are frightened and in survival mode. This was obviously this hostage's brief.

I called him to come out to me, but he didn't move. I repeated my demand again, and he slowly came out toward me. Once he was with me, we searched him and then grilled him for who he was and what he knew. He was definitely a hostage, and confirmed that there was at least one offender in the building. He also told us there were seven hostages in total. We told him to stay where he was and that we would be back for him, then set off to clear the rest of the building.

The other hostages were all located in various places around the block. They were secreted in among shelving units, in cupboards, or sitting in a fetal position somewhere more prominent. Some were unresponsive, others overly talkative, and the rest actively compliant. After we had found no more offenders, we went back to get our hostages. Except they weren't there. As per their brief, they had all wandered off and rehidden. We spent a frustrating extra 10 minutes rounding them all up, did a head count and then marched them all out, using ourselves as a shield around them.

Mission two complete. We carried out a further two rescues on two other buildings, with much the same results. One had an IED (improvised explosive device) set up in it, which I unknowingly stepped over to get from A to B. I didn't even notice it, so intent was I on identifying people and not objects.

The day ended later in the afternoon. I was absolutely stuffed. We had been on our feet all day, and under maximum stress for a prolonged period of time. It was mentally and physically draining. We were all soaked with sweat, but had completed our missions as directed. We were looking forward to having the night off. Throughout the course, we had routinely got up at 5 a.m., completed an hour of physical activity before breakfast, then gone right through to 10 p.m. Having Saturday night off was a welcome relief.

My next progress report was on the Sunday night, and it was shit. Mr Incredible brought up my entry issues; but, by now, after my week of being watched continually, I just felt anger at his lecture and utterly sick of being his focus. Like a sullen child, I sat there while he talked to me in his infuriating sympathetic voice, wishing he'd just yell. *Yes, yes, yes*, I nodded and agreed. Right. Moving on.

Throughout the course and around the environs of Police College, GB and I had got a few smiles and supportive looks, mainly from female recruits. I presumed it was the fact that we were the only girls on our course. Wherever we turned we had a positive group of well-wishers, which was nice. However, the flip side was that when you were tired and grumpy, being stared at or talked to by strangers became stifling.

Standing in the food queue at each meal break, I could hear people commenting on us – all nice comments, of course, but comments nonetheless. After a while, I risked being thought of as an antisocial bugger by 'forgetting' to remove my balaclava after an exercise and while I was moving on to the next one. With it off, passers-by often tried to make eye contact and talk to me. With the balaclava on, I was avoided like the plague.

Monday spelt the beginning of the last week. The course was the best course I had ever done in the police, but my two weeks of being watched constantly was wearing thin. I was looking forward to getting home.

One thing that I would normally look forward to was to happen in the last week. A helicopter trip. We were to be taught the 'getting on' and 'getting off' techniques, as helicopters are often used for deployments when there is no quicker way of getting to the job. During my time in the Air Force, I had managed to get lots of trips around in an Iroquois. I had been dropped into Lyttelton Harbour from one, taken into the middle of nowhere and left to survive for three days in another, been aboard during contour flying, and many other general sorties.

This week, however, I was neither looking forward to nor feeling enthused about the prospect of the trip. Over the previous two weeks, I had often felt nauseous due to tiredness, the everlasting flu that I still had, and bad nutrition. This, combined with my tendency to regularly get motion sickness, meant I had managed to talk myself into getting crook as soon as we took off. To top it all off, it was blowing like 40 bastards and the rain was coming in sideways. I guess it was not really a fear of flying that I had. It was a fear of crashing. Helicopters sometimes crashed. People died. I did not want to die.

While waiting for my ride in the death machine, I tried to keep warm by parking myself under some pampas grass that was growing out of a bank. It was raining and I was propped up in full AOS kit – body armour, wet-weather gear, slung M4, over-vest, helmet and goggles. With my eyes open I could just peep out from under the grass, but while standing there in its shelter I closed my eyes in the hope I would fall asleep. I nearly did, but was disturbed by laughter. GB, who was doing much the same thing as I was beside me, had watched quietly and without warning me as one of the guys had sneaked up on us and captured our nodding-off-in-the-bush moment for posterity. It remains one of my nicest memories of the course: a relaxing moment with GB, doing what horses do – sleeping without falling over.

All too soon the helicopter landed and I was ordered out of my bush and over to the shuddering, thundering contraption. I scrabbled inside quickly so I wouldn't get stuck with the ghastly outer seat (the doors weren't going to be closed, and the outside seat gave you no protection from falling – oh, except for the tiny useless seatbelt we wore, of course). Mr Incredible wedged himself in beside me on the outside, so I was sandwiched in the middle.

As soon as we took off, I shut my eyes. I sneaked them open at one point, just as the pilot tipped the machine to one side, allowing me an uninterrupted view of my imminent death – sharp rocks with white caps breaking over them, a matter of metres below. We were flying over a cliff face, and just at the time I looked, a gust of wind hit the helicopter and shot us off to one side in a terrifyingly uncontrolled movement.

I didn't waste my precious final few seconds before crashing by thinking about mundane matters. Instead, I began to think about who would come to my funeral. I immediately hoped that people I didn't like wouldn't turn up and pretend they knew me well. These same people would probably eat all the nice cucumber sandwiches that hopefully someone else would have had the forethought to make. If cucumber wasn't in season, I would be happy with asparagus rolls. Don't they actually come in season at the same time, though? Both would need really fresh bread and lashings of butter. Not margarine. Nothing says more clearly that your life hasn't been worth much than using margarine instead of butter. That would just cheapen my existence.

I wasn't given much time to contemplate all this, though. The jolt back to reality came quite quickly as, after righting the helicopter, the pilot took us around a point and we landed in a little cove. As soon as the skids touched down, we all scrambled out to the safety of dry land. I was relieved to be out. I think Mr Incredible was, too, as he gave me an impromptu hug. I made a mental note of it – if it ever looked like I was going to fail the course, I should mention the cuddle.

All that was left to do now was wait for the rest of our section to arrive. We now had a small navigation exercise to embark on, combined with rural patrolling. At the end of it, again, we would be piled into the helicopter and taken back to College.

Rural patrolling is an enjoyable part of the many skills we were taught. Each person in the patrol has a different role. It is tiring, as you are forever on high alert, waiting for a threat to pop up in front of you; plus you're walking and sometimes running along in full kit. You are constantly aware of and assessing your use of cover, the best escape route if compromised and, of course, where it is exactly you're supposed to be heading. The training we had done should all be starting to combine into the skills required. My navigation was pretty awful, so I was fortunate – as was everyone else – that I wasn't given this role. I knew with that certainty I often possess that I would get us lost.

We set off at a jaunty pace. Over the next couple of hours, our navigator successfully manoeuvred us into our required spot. On time, a helicopter landed, we all climbed aboard and were whisked back to College. The weather hadn't improved any but we still hadn't crashed, and despite my terror of falling out of the aircraft, I believed that my survival meant I had been given another chance at life, so it was time to make the most of it. I *would* make it to the end of the course.

7

THE LONGEST NIGHT

When I had grilled my husband for details of the qualifying course, he had nonchalantly told me about the last exercise you did. It kicked off in the early evening of the Wednesday night and continued through the night, finishing mid-morning on the Thursday. He hadn't given it much air-time, and dismissed it as 'great to be finished afterwards'. In hindsight, I'm glad he didn't warn me about it. Like every other exercise we did, it would be a necessary evil; and not knowing just *how* evil it was stood me in better stead for finishing it.

As Wednesday arrived, I was simply gratified to still be there. We had lost three people so far off the course, for varying things. Two of those three were in our section. I felt jinxed. Our original eight was now six. It was definitely not too late to be next.

The afternoon prior to the exercise, we received a full briefing. The scenario was that a splinter group of religious zealots was making threats with firearms. The main threat was from a self-styled leader; the informant was one of the group who had escaped. They believed their leader was now taking it too far and appeared to be losing it mentally, so the one who had escaped had informed the police. Now our mission was to locate and secure the group without any loss of life. They lived very remotely, and it would take some time to walk in. A whole night, in fact. Now there was a surprise.

We set off at 6 p.m. that night from Police College in minivans. We all wore full kit as well as carrying our Glocks in thigh holsters, and in our hands we each carried an old .223 long arm, which was no longer operational equipment for New Zealand police.

GB and I had gone nuts with the food we were carrying. We'd been shopping on our one day off (the previous Sunday), and had bought every imaginable energy-snack-like treat we could find. A guy on the course also had a giant-jelly-bean contact. He had something like 15 kilos of jelly beans, so I (of course) bought 5 kilos off him.

I mixed some of these giant jelly beans with a scroggin mix I had purchased, then put everything in little dinky snap-lock bags in my over-vest. When I had filled up the front pocket, which was immediately accessible, I found a rear pocket and put the rest of my snacks in there. I would need a helper to access this area, but figured I would do this when we stopped for a break. I also had beer sticks (mini salami sausages generally more at home on a bar leaner next to a beer-swilling male), which I had never taken before but which I thought would be a nice change from all the sweet snacks I usually ate, muesli bars, electrolyte-replacement drinks, bananas and chocolate. I also carried protein bars in case I ran out of everything else. In total I had perhaps 5 kilos of food. For one night's walk. There's nothing like being prepared.

Our starting point was an extremely remote location, which was high and exposed. Our four sections were divided into two groups – mine and GB's were combined. The other two sections peeled off to another location to start, and we were taken to our start point. We would all be walking in to a common location where the baddies were holed up, but from different directions. The weather was foul again, like on our helicopter day, and horizontal sleet greeted me as soon as I rolled out of the van, managing to drive straight into my joints. Shortly after arriving we all set out in the pitch-black, in our sections, and the longest night of my life began.

I was soaked through to my core within five minutes of walking. I was wearing tactical gloves on my hands, which weren't the least bit capable of holding out water, and once waterlogged were probably not very tactical. I could scarcely feel the firearm I was holding, and early on resorted to cradling it. As the rain came down on me, I tried to keep my head tucked into my chest to stop the driving shards hitting my face. To protect my eyes, which were getting stung, I pulled my goggles down. They immediately fogged up. Either way I couldn't see where the fuck I was going. This sucked. Big-time.

My hands began aching from the cold and my dexterity was rapidly becoming next to nothing. I was only half an hour in, and already I couldn't give a stuff who saw my incorrect muzzle awareness. I began longing for a broken ankle. If I fell and hurt myself seriously enough, I would, hopefully, have done enough to get me through the course; plus, I wouldn't have to endure any more of this beastly Wellington weather.

But as luck would have it, my ankles were as strong as an ox's. They held me up through the bumpy tracks, steep hills, potholes and everywhere in between. One thing that was often talked about in the AOS courses was 'stress' injuries. They could also have been called 'Clayton's injuries' – the injury you get when you're not really injured. The injury that appears when you are in fact just too tired to go on. That's why I hung out for a snapping limb. There was no way that would be mistaken for a Hollywood. Ideally I needed a large piece of bone to be jutting out from my leg to convince everyone it was real and that I wasn't fibbing.

Regardless of my desires, I kept trudging forward with the rest of my team, although in the dark I really had no idea who was who. They were all just vague, shadowy figures. We were walking in a staggered line formation, with Mr Incredible continually coming up to the middle from the back, popping into position just behind me. Thinking he was one of us, I would realign myself with him and then he would tell me to get in formation again. I should have guessed it was him from the silhouette of his chin. Grumbling to myself, I would either drop back or trot forward, wishing that Mr Incredible would just sod off.

As the hours rolled by, I began to feel quite fatigued. I was wet to the core, cold, and felt the lack of sleep and the long hours over the last three weeks building up. We were all steadily making our way across the top of a mountain range, heading toward a gully. Once we hit the gully, we would be winding our way inland and meeting up with the other team, who would have approached from the opposite direction. Little did I know then how long this would take us.

By about midnight – five hours walking without stopping – I paused in my stride when I saw what I believed were torch lights up ahead. They were small bright lights bobbing around, and I thought they might have been on the road that was around the corner about half a kilometre in front. At my call, we all hunkered down behind cover, passed the NVGs (night-vision goggles) around, then sent forward a couple of scouts to have a closer look around the next corner.

Nothing was spotted, so up we got and set off walking once more. A short time later, I thought I saw the lights again. This time I didn't call an immediate halt, but just squinted into the gloom. Then I blinked and looked around me. Every direction I looked in, I saw more lights. They were everywhere. Like lots of people waving small torches in the hills around me. It dawned on me what was happening. I think my eyeballs had taken such a beating from the earlier rain that they were now conjuring up spots. Lots of them. Realising how my earlier hallucination had halted a whole section – well, actually two sections – and feeling somewhat embarrassed by this, I didn't call any more lights in.

During this course, one thing both GB and I had found is that police-issue AOS overalls are not at all accommodating for female toiletry habits. The overalls have a vertical zipper that opens from either end – mighty handy if you are a boy with a bendy appendage, but we were not boys. To access the required part of the female anatomy needed for bladder evacuation we had to remove the over-vest, ballistic vest, belt with Glock, wet-weather gear, and then the overalls. I needed a She-P. I had read about them, but didn't have one. I won't gross you out by describing it here. Go Google it. You will understand.

I managed to hang on until after midnight before deciding I would need to take the next opportunity to pee. I began mentally preparing for this exercise. When we were finally allowed to stop for a 10-minute break, I took my chance while the rest of the section refuelled.

I nipped off over a couple of small hills and scouted around until I found a suitable bush. Although it was pitch-black, we had a couple of sets of NVGs in our group and a couple of comedians in my section. I didn't want to tempt fate. My mission now was not to lose any of the kit I had to take off in the dark, and to somehow retain my dignity. Once I had shed my layers, with a sigh of relief I crouched down, semi-naked in the darkness – and sat squarely on a gorse bush.

I winced in pain, shot up about a metre in the air, then peed on the sleeve of my overalls. Bloody stupid overalls! Bloody stupid gorse! Bloody stupid pee! Pouring water from my bottle onto the sleeve was an issue, as it had a bite-valve attached. It needed a suction motion to pour. The small amount that managed to dribble out got rid of part of the problem, but I now had a saturated arm. There was nothing I could do about it, other than cope. I struggled back into the rest of my kit and went to rejoin my section.

Having an empty bladder now, I felt it was safe to keep drinking water. That's the crazy thing about inadequate equipment such as overalls that you can't go to the toilet in. Up until then I had risked dehydrating just so I didn't have to go through this debacle in the first place.

After the walk, GB told me she had come across the same

THE LONGEST NIGHT

difficulty. Not being able to readily go 'number ones', she had also used our one and only stop to accommodate it. I don't think she peed on herself, though.

We came across a couple of contacts along the way. One incident began as an explosion, triggered by a trip-wire across the road we were walking on. We all dropped to the ground at the bang, trying to find any targets in the darkness; but on not finding anyone, we had to continue walking forward at a crawl. The trip-wire had been put in as a warning by the offenders – they knew we were on our way and the explosion would tell them exactly how far away we were.

The next contact was less loud. As we crept forward in the darkness, a guy jumped up from where he had been sitting on the side of the road, asking us loudly who we were and where we were going. He was dealt with quickly and painlessly – challenge, comply, handcuff, move on.

By now we had reached the lowest part of the walk geographically, having come down into a valley that led to the coast. We now had to travel up a gully to our main contact point. And the entire route was up a stream bed that was flowing with water.

When we first set off from the beginning of the gully, we started by crossing the small stream a few times, but before long the track consistently ran up the stream bed. Those who sought to keep their boots dry soon gave up. Twenty minutes in, my feet were as wet as my sleeve. They also probably looked like they felt: wrinkled, white and as cold as ice. Not stopping was good as it didn't give your body a chance to cool down.

Relentlessly we trudged on, and it was then that I began to find what a complete waste of time bringing in 5 kilos of food had been. I hadn't eaten any of the stuff in the rear pocket, as all my stopping time (when everyone else had eaten) had been taken up with peeing on myself. I could now only use the readily accessed stuff in the front pocket of my vest, which was nuts and scroggin.

It turned out I hated the nuts and scroggin. Try going for a light run while downing dried fruit and nuts – you'll find that when you try to suck in a breath, little bits of nut will shoot down your airway, causing you to choke. It's not a good food when carrying out stealthy approaches. In among the nuts and dried fruit, however, were the blessed giant jelly beans. Whenever I felt myself flag under the continued effort of wading up a cold, rocky and uneven stream bed – every couple of hundred metres or so – I would reward myself with a giant jelly bean. It gave me a tremendous physical and psychological lift.

I often thought about stopping. Despite the jelly beans I was getting a bit sick of this exercise, as you might have read between the lines. We had now been walking non-stop for eight hours, apart from the bit where someone had tried to blow us up and the 10-minute food break, and I was well over walking in streams.

Then I thought of GB. To my knowledge I hadn't passed her in the dark, so she was up ahead somewhere with her section. If she could keep going, I could keep going. She told me later that she'd thought the same thing when she had wanted to stop.

Finally, at about 5 a.m., we arrived at our target. It was a woolshed in the middle of nowhere. The second group had approached from the other direction, and they told us later that although they'd had less ground to cover (and no streams), their journey was straight up and straight down, and was extremely physical. Maybe our streams hadn't been so bad after all.

We all took up our designated observation points, and laid up to wait for the contact to be made. Then the smell of bacon began filling our nostrils. I lifted my head from where it rested against my arm and, looking over my firearm at the shed, tried to figure out whether I was imagining things. *Who the hell is cooking bacon?*

It seemed to be coming from the woolshed. What torture! As I lay there, waiting for the other sections to get into position, I felt the chill begin to creep into my bones through my wet clothes. I began shivering violently and uncontrollably. God, I was cold. My teeth were clacking together like an old typewriter, and my whole body shook. I hoped I wouldn't have to engage a target, as it would be a miracle if I could hit anything smaller than the large building directly in front of me.

I remained there with my section for perhaps 40 minutes. My vantage point wasn't the best, as the likely exit from the building for the offenders was on the side that had a door – and this was the opposite side to where I was. So I just lay there, shaking and chattering, wriggling my legs to get some circulation going and feeling really sorry for myself. All the while, the delicious smells of a fry-up filled the fresh morning air.

Then – perhaps when the bacon had finished cooking – the sound of shotgun blasts shattered the silence. My body tensed up, and I craned my head to see if I could see anything. Nope. Not a thing. As I'd predicted, all the action was on the side opposite to where we were holed up. The group that had climbed mountains all night had been rewarded for their physical prowess and had got to participate fully. They were busy engaging an offender who had appeared on their side, presented a shotgun at nothing in particular, then let off a couple of rounds. It was all over soon. And I hadn't even *seen* the bad guys.

I did meet them afterward, however. They were also our cooks, and the delicious smells we had been subjected to were coming from our breakfast, which they had been cooking while they waited for us to storm their stronghold. Once inside the shed, I nipped into a small room off the main shearing shed, and changed out of my cold, wet clothes and into warm thermals. I began dreaming about my warm shower back at Police College.

After a good breakfast, we were told to put all our kit back on and prepare to walk out. A 10-minute stroll, I wondered? Nope. A one-and-a-half-hour hump up a mountain. Just what I felt like. It was about 8 a.m. by now and I was craving sleep, not more exercise.

Within about three minutes of walking up the vertical track, I was drenched in sweat. Despite the torrential rain of the previous evening, today the sun came out; then, finally, like a desert mirage, our vans appeared in front of us. We gratefully clambered into them. All the way back to Police College I dozed, dreaming of my imminent shower and the end of the course.

Once back, we were only given a couple of hours before our next timing, which was weapons cleaning. I collapsed into my bed, grateful for whatever shut-eye I could get. At the chirping of the infernal alarm clock, I again got into overalls and headed up to the firearms range. It was then that we found out we'd lost one more applicant from the overnighter. Like the others before him, he was whisked off when no one was looking. As we cleaned weapons, I pondered my fate. It clearly wasn't going to be over until the fat lady sang.

That night brought the final activity of the whole course. The formal dinner. A celebration of those previous three weeks of hard work – although you had no way of telling that you weren't still being watched and assessed. We dressed up in our uniforms and were whisked off to a nearby yacht club to feast, tell tall stories and drink nice wine. We were all tickled pink that we had finished, and after a few drinks and back-slaps, settled in for a night of celebrating. I was mainly just looking forward to eating something that didn't come in a crinkly wrapper with 'energy' written somewhere on it.

After dinner, we sat and listened to a guest speaker. I don't think anyone had told him that there were two females on the course, though. He was a policing veteran with close to 250 years of experience, and ex-AOS. He regaled us with a few good stories, took the mickey out of a couple of the instructors, and then got into the important role we were about to embark on – as fully fledged AOS members. But clearly he wasn't able to adapt his speech 'off the cuff' – GB and I sat there uncomfortably at first, then silently fuming as he spoke of 'your wives and girlfriends supporting you', 'all you men', and a multitude of other comments clearly designed for a male-only audience. A couple of times he even looked directly at me as he made these comments, and although it took some effort in my tired state, I was able to bite back the temptation to shout, 'Hello! Two of us are girls!'

At the end of the night, we travelled back to College and collapsed into bed, knackered. The next morning we had a final debrief (during which Mr Incredible could have said anything to me he wanted – I didn't care, as long as he said I'd passed), and were given the handshake, certificate and photo that said we had passed.

I had finally done it – and oh, that fat mamma could sing her giant mammaries off now! I was finished! Finally, after many years of hoping and dreaming, here I was – an operational Armed Offenders Squad member in the New Zealand Police. I felt like I had won Lotto.

8

OPERATIONAL

When I got back home I was very excited about what the future was going to hold, and also a little nervous about the first call-outs and how they would combine with family life. Enter, the Newtons. They're our close friends, and with the amount of time we all spent together it was like we were one big family unit.

The Newton family consists of Mum (Tosca), Dad (Tim) and two teenage daughters (Kristie and Melissa). By now my son was at school, so the routine was that Tosca (or 'Mummy Tosca' as my son would call her when he was very little) would pick him up for us, and I or my husband would call round after work to collect him. I would usually find him curled up on a couch with one of the girls, telling tall tales or eating something. It almost felt wrong to remove him and take him back to our quiet, three-person house. As time went on, the Newtons became an integral part of our AOS life and our ability to both be able to work on the squad. They were there for us if the pager went off at an odd time, or during the workday, or if we had a couple of days away – although this rarely happened, as generally one of us would stay back to keep some sort of normality to family life.

During a workday call-out, often while racing to the squad room, I would be calling Tosca or Tim and warning them what was happening so that if it dragged on, I knew my son would be picked up and very well cared for and, most importantly, be surrounded by a loving family. I usually had them telling me to shut up and get off the phone as it would all be sorted, so not to worry. And it always was sorted.

We worked out back-up plans and SOPs (standard operating procedures) for how we would manage all this over multiple combined Newton/Williams family dinners. Knowing that it would work out, I could now concentrate on the job at hand – getting a few call-outs under my belt.

As a now-legitimate squad member, I felt 2 metres tall and bulletproof and was itching to get going. I was also keenly aware of not wanting to look incompetent in front of the existing squad members. Being conscious that I wasn't the best AOS member ever to have graduated from Police College – in fact, on a very, very good day I would describe myself as just about scratching up to average – meant that I had a lot to prove, both to myself and to the rest of the team.

Some of the guys on the squad I had now joined were naturals from the get-go. They had intuition, quick decision-making ability and natural, harnessed aggression. I didn't have any of those characteristics in abundance, and certainly didn't harbour unrealistic dreams of instantly locating them in my previously forgotten top pocket on the first call-out. But I did not want to be thought of as not a very good operator early on, and knew I needed time in the saddle to work on what I believed were my weaknesses. I was also somewhat desperate to let them know that having the first female on a squad in Central Districts was a step forward, not a crazy clerical error made by someone who got drunk at work one day and accidentally ticked the wrong box. (And no, I am not suggesting that our HR department drinks on duty. In fact, I would be offended if they did, as I've never been invited over.)

The squad members I would be working with would have adopted processes gained from years of operational experience, and

I would now have to try to integrate myself with them without looking and acting like a completely useless twat. My first job, however, wasn't a problem. I got to stare at a brick wall for 40 minutes.

The pager had gone off in the wee small hours. I leapt up, feeling disbelief at the fact I was going on a call-out and terror at what I might have to actually do. I roared into the station, leaving my husband to 'hold the baby', who was by now school age; we'd decided to leave the Newtons alone for the first call-out. When I got to the squad room, I tried to look at everyone else to see what their order of getting kit together was. It didn't help much, though, as everyone had their own unique way. I would have to make it up myself.

Naturally, the first thing was my overalls. Without trying to make a spectacle of myself, I whipped my pants down, revealing not my flashest set of undies, and wriggled into the overalls. Next, boots. Next, Glock thigh holster. Now, what about a Glock? I had to wait until the last man had kitted up to see who wasn't there and take theirs, as I didn't yet have one assigned specifically to me. In the meantime, instead of standing hopefully under the Glock rack, I moved on.

Body armour. This had caused me some concern during the three-week qualifying course. I had gone down to the course with the retiring inspector's body armour, which was way too big and meant that when I was walking uphill the armour hit against the top of my thighs, giving me the added difficulty of a leg-raise exercise during hill climbs. But at the beginning of the second week, I had received a brand spanking new set of small body armour. If I stuffed up the course, there was no way they would be able to return it after I'd sweated all over it, and it would be too little for anyone else on the squad to wear. It cost $4000, and I didn't think they'd be happy carrying that cost for nothing. So, for the second and third weeks of qualifying, I had an added financial pressure to pass.

Thankfully, as I had got through, I was lucky enough to be sporting this very new armour, complete with willy protector (a flap that hangs down over your nether regions and protects the large, pulsating artery in your groin) and shoulder guards – which gave me a width that equalled my height. It messed up my hair somewhat, though; whenever I tugged it over my head, my hair was pulled out of the band that held it. When the armour was on, the shoulder guards made it impossible to reach up to spruce up the do, so during every call-out I would end up looking like Worzel Gummidge.

Next, I put on my balaclava. This was flame-retardant and quite a heavy fabric, and wasn't the most comfortable thing to wear operationally. I then had another hiatus – I was to use a left-over radio, but as staff were still arriving I had to wait to see what the leftovers would be. So I continued on with my over-vest. This was bloody heavy. All my munitions were in this, as well as my wet-weather gear in the large rear pocket. Prior to my qualifying course, I had sat down on the floor of our lounge with a large needle and thread and reduced the length of the old over-vest I had acquired, as, like the old armour I had used, it hung too low. As a safety and surface worker in my earlier Air Force role (the painting planes and packing safety equipment job), one part of my trade had been heavy harness work, and this assisted me greatly. The four layers of fabric and leather I sewed through on the over-vest were not the prettiest when completed, but functioned more than adequately.

By now, everyone who was attending the call-out had arrived, so I scurried over and nabbed a left-over Glock, M4 and radio. I was ready. I think.

Like on the first day of school, I hovered around and waited to see who went with who; then, seeing a free space, I jumped in the AOS truck. On the way, the AOS boss, who was driving, called another squad out – our numbers were too low to do the job safely. The nearest squad was at Wanganui, so shortly after we left Palmerston North, they would be getting woken up too. Now we were off. I felt nervous in anticipation of what I was about to do. Our trip was about 30 minutes to a small central North Island police station close to where the incident was; on the way, I was mentally running over my drills. I was also chatting to the AOS boss, whom I knew, which was a good way to calm my nerves. The rest of the guys were in cars following us, or sandwiched into the back of the truck we were in.

When we got there, we piled out and went straight into the police station to wait for the other squad to arrive. As we waited, I tried to act as nonchalantly as possible, as if this wasn't my very first call-out. As if I didn't have a fluttering moth kicking up merry hell in my stomach. As if I did this every day.

The second squad arrived about 20 minutes later. As they walked in, all clad in their black with balaclavas on, I had no idea who was who. I had done my qualifying course with one AOS guy from Wanganui, but couldn't pick him out from the crowd. We were given an initial briefing by the local staff. A member of a local gang had been seen with a firearm, and was now holed up in the gang headquarters. We had no idea how many people were in the place, no idea about dogs and, aside from the aforementioned firearm, no idea about any other weapons. We were, however, aware that the place was well fortified. Entry would be interesting.

After the initial briefing, the local police staff left the room and we received a second AOS brief, where we were given our assigned tasks. As the other squad had had to travel the furthest, they were given the best job – the front of the address. This was desirable, as when entry was finally able to be made they would most likely be the ones doing it. The other roles were cordon only. Cordon, as the name suggests, is the team that surrounds the house; then the entry team sweeps in and clears it.

My assigned area was to one side of the address, along with F, another experienced guy from my station. On 'Go!', we rolled into our spot with the other members of the team. With my heart pounding so loud that I could hear it in my ears, I ran to my designated area and braced myself for action.

I was greeted by a large, impenetrable brick wall. Aside from a big front-end loader bursting forth from within (which I guess could never be entirely discounted), there wasn't going to be too much happening for me in the next 40 minutes. I scanned it carefully in the hope that there was a hidden door someone might be flushed out of; an emergency escape hatch, perhaps, or a trapdoor hidden by the long grass. But there was nothing. Just bricks. And long grass.

From where F and I were positioned, the entrance was to our right. As we stood there gazing at absolutely nothing, an entry plan was being formulated, then approved, over the earpiece poked deep into the waxy depths of my ear canal. I turned my head to one side, straining to listen, hopeful of hearing my name being offered forth to bolster entry-team numbers. But I heard nothing. I was staying on wall duty. Shortly afterward, I heard a succession of loud bangs, then explosions, then a whole lot of yelling. I could hear the sound of running feet, more yelling, and then crashing. All the while, my eyes were as big as saucers, my pulse was racing, my hands were shaking, and I thought I might like to go to the toilet right then and there. In my pants, if need be.

After what seemed like an eternity, it was announced that one male was coming out. The earpiece crackling into life sometimes gives you a fright. You're lost in your world of thought, and suddenly there is this previously forgotten voice in your ear. In my case, it was muffled by the wax.

As the male came into my peripheral vision, I heard another squad member to my rear and right yelling instructions to him. The offender was directed to a safe area, where he was handcuffed and searched. As he was being debriefed, another male was brought out to the same location. I half-turned in their direction to see who our targets were. A couple of weedy little guys stared back at me, their eyes about as big as mine had been. They had been asleep, and had been woken by the entry team entering. Loudly. Chances were they had done something in their pants.

A subsequent search of the property turned up a firearm, and that was that. House cleared. Guns found. Targets neutralised. Move on. Unceremoniously, it was all over. I now had one job under my belt. I was now experienced. *Next*.

9

ANGRY MEN IN WEE VILLAGES

Just like the days when I had worked on the PNT, many of the AOS call-outs I went on were to small, outlying villages, to deal with belligerent and obnoxious males. In 2008, my family and I were booked to fly to France on a Saturday in the middle of the New Zealand winter. This isn't all that relevant to the job I'm now going to tell you about, but I thought you'd like to know that I went to France all through a New Zealand winter. It was very hot. Back home, you had the worst weather in a 10-year history. I don't speak French, but I learned that waiters shouldn't be called garçon. That means boy, not waiter. Girl waiters are offended by being called garçon.

One great thing about policing is how leave accrues and the fact that you can take a large chunk of it all at one time and do something as momentous as having an amazing family holiday. This was also a way for us as a family to just be together – no interruptions from work or others. Our son got to have us all to himself for two whole months, and for me it was a chance to not feel guilty that he had to spend time with anyone else. Getting completely away from criminals and their irritating ways was an added bonus. Police work can be somewhat draining, and a clean break away from all it entails is an excellent way to recharge the batteries.

Anyway, on the day before we were due to take off overseas to accidentally insult French female waiters, I received a call from the AOS boss asking if I was available for a last job before I flew out. Hell, yes. One day before hitting the skyways, I got to have a last *yippee*. In a small outlying village, naturally, with a belligerent and obnoxious local.

The call-out started at 5.30 a.m. We all assembled in the squad room, sorted kit out, and loaded up vans and cars. The initial intell we had about the job was extremely brief, but we would be getting a further, detailed briefing at the small station we were heading to.

On the way over, I sang to my colleagues: 'I'm leav-ing, on a jet plane . . . don't know when I'll be back again . . .' They asked me what would happen to my ticket on the jet plane if the job turned into a two-day siege, or I got shot. I hadn't really thought that far ahead; I'd just wanted to have a last job before I went. The thought that it might prevent me from going on the holiday of a lifetime was not something I had considered. Thinking about it while we drove, I decided I didn't care what happened, or what state I would travel in, but travel I would.

When we arrived, we received the more detailed briefing. Our offender was a gang associate – now there was a surprise – and he had taken a firearm to a family gathering and presented it. Sounded just like the sort of family gathering I would want to avoid. The information the local detective had was that the target was still in possession of the firearm. After this general briefing, we gathered into our squad for a second briefing, this one focusing on how we would carry out our deployment.

In my section, I was given the front of the address together with one other – G. This was great. Front doors are, not surprisingly, at the front of addresses, and it was probable that this would be the way the offender would have to come out. I had now been on the squad for about six months and was getting a good variety of areas to cover on each call-out. Front was my preferred spot. After each section had sorted out entry tactics, I was given a small extendable ladder. If there were fences to climb, this would be helpful. We all piled into our vehicles, and set off to the address.

When we arrived, as soon as the vehicle slowed we all piled out and got our bearings. Along with G, I took off at a fast walk. As we turned into the street in question, we could see the target address in the gloomy morning light up ahead. It was down the far end of the street, on the opposite side of the road to us.

The first property we came to on our side of the road afforded excellent protection from being seen. It had a huge front garden and lawn area, and the entire street frontage was overgrown with trees and shrubs. As we got to the gate, G and I slipped inside and continued making our way down the section, across the mossy lawn, under cover the whole way. Part-way down, however, my earpiece crackled into life: 'Our target has come out of his house. He's looking up and down the street. He seems to know we're here. Someone get in a position to challenge him now!'

Neither G nor I was close enough at the time. We sped up to try to reach the corner of the property quicker, hearing further information about what the target was now doing. When we got to the area closest to where his house was, we both cut in through the shrubbery. 'Whoever is opposite, he's looking in to where you are,' the voice in my earpiece announced. Whoever had eyes on the front of the address was relaying what they could see. I froze, my foot poised in the air, a low-hanging branch threatening to whip back upon my passing. Shit.

Ahead of me, G was poised in the same frozen motion. We might have just been compromised. It's not healthy when they know where *you* are but you have no idea where *they* are. Our dense foliage cover was so good that we couldn't see through it to where he apparently was.

'Someone get in and challenge him! He's moving around the front of the property still! He's gone over near the car and seems to be fumbling around with something near the gate.'

Next thing I heard the challenge: 'Armed police! Get your hands in the air! Armed police! Get your hands in the air!' I crashed forward through the bushes so that I was right up to the front fence – the need to stay silent no longer important – and could now see our target. He was standing on a concrete footpath outside his house, wearing bare feet, shorts and no shirt. He was the man we were looking for.

Bringing my M4 up into position, I trained the aim point (a small red dot of light that is the sight of the firearm) on him, and watched him as he just stood there, nervously watching the team approaching him from my left. His feet were twitching and turning this way and that. The other team had to expose themselves from cover and move across toward the front of the property to get close enough to take him out if required. Their angle of approach wasn't ideal, but the offender had forced this approach through his actions.

While I continued to watch, the target brought his fists and fingers up in the typical gang gesture that showed defiance and whole-hearted non-compliance. He had decided to overcome his nervousness with aggression. 'Fuck you! Fuck you!' he shouted at the team challenging him. He moved around in a tight circle of about a metre radius – defiant, but not stupid enough to fully force the issue – taunting the team to 'Come on then! Shoot me! Shoot me!' His arms were now held outward from his body, in a not entirely genuine suggestion of openness.

The team kept yelling at him and he continued yelling at them. No one was close enough to physically take him to the ground, and the front door of the house, which was still open, was directly behind him, thereby opening up a large area of possible threat to the contact team should they move in front of it. It was still too risky to close up the gap. As all this was going down, I was still half in the bushes, my firearm poking through and the red dot on his chest. What was he going to do?

They continued trying to negotiate with him from where they stood; in my earpiece, the boss was now calling upon someone to either spray him or take him down. Neither of these requests could be actioned due to where the offender was standing. The next command yelled at him was to get on the ground. Watching him through my sights, waving his arms and still yelling, I willed him to just *do* what he was getting told to.

I could see he was in a quandary. While looking at the contact team telling him to get down, he was also glancing down at the dew-covered early-morning ground. It became clear to me that he was weighing up lying on this cold, hard surface against getting shot. To get wet, or not to get wet? Is it more important to stay dry and get shot? Not a hard decision to make in my book, but it was fair to say there weren't too many similarities between his way of thinking and mine. Finally, he turned toward the open front door and yelled to someone inside to get his clothes for him. He wasn't going to do a thing until he was fully dressed!

Miraculously, a female appeared holding a pile of clothes. The moment the contact team saw her, she was yelled at to get her hands in the air – but she seemed equally as well versed at doing her own thing in her own time, as she also chose to ignore their orders and disappeared back inside, empty-handed.

The target casually put on the shirt he had been given, then got down on his knees, then stomach, arms outstretched, and face down. As soon as he was horizontal, members of the contact team pounced on him and dragged him off to an area away from the obviously occupied house, where it was safer for them to deal with him.

Negotiations were then started with the remaining members of the house to come out, one by one. Despite the earlier ignoring of instructions, this time it was done easily and the woman was brought over to the same area as the offender. They both sat there while the entry team moved in and checked the house for further occupants. I kept my eyes glued to the address while they did this, waiting for someone to perhaps pop out a window. But there was no one else home.

The inquiry team then came forward. These were the local police staff, who would take over the arrest- and search-procedures. Our job had been solely to arrest the target and clear the house of people. The first area of search was the place near the gate where the offender had been fumbling around as we were getting into position.

About a minute into the search, the AOS commander was called over by the search team. They had found, hanging under the edge of the fence, obscured from view but not from the offender's searching hands, a sawn-off .22 firearm. On further inspection, it was found to have a loaded magazine attached and one bullet chambered.

We found out later that he'd told police he thought we were members of an opposing gang turning up. He never talked about the firearm, but, gangs being gangs, it didn't take a great imagination to guess what he was going to do with the loaded one he was reaching for. Right then and there, I made a decision: next time I had a decent overseas holiday planned, I would *not* be attending any last-minute jobs. And France was wonderful, thanks for asking.

10

MOVING ON

By early 2008, I had spent 10 years as a detective in the CIB at Palmerston North. Was I still happy with what I was doing? Well, to be perfectly frank, no. I had enjoyed the year of both applying for and getting into the AOS, but now that I was there, every other part of policing seemed to hold no interest for me. The next positions available to me were promotion within the CIB, or leaving to go back to the uniform branch — either as a sergeant or simply as a uniformed constable.

We had a shortage of detective sergeants in the CIB at this time, so senior detectives were given roles as relieving detective sergeants, which meant running squads. I, consistently, wasn't one of them, and this made me feel conspicuous.

I had only just gone back to full-time hours after my son had started school, and I was constantly feeling pressure that I wasn't there enough as a parent. Both of us were working 40-plus hours a week, with call-outs on top of that. In fact, my husband and I had an AOS call-out on our child's first pet day so we missed it, as did he. Actually, that affected us parents more than the dog and the child. I don't think our son knew what had happened aside from the fact that he got to hang out with his second family the Newtons for the morning. As it was rather a frantic, unscheduled 'our pagers have gone off' drop-off at their house, the dog had to accompany him. While we skulked around in someone's backyard for two hours, they both got to eat lollies and watch TV. That was probably why the dog defecated inside their house, come to think of it — he was an outdoor dog and must have got carried away with the excitement of being inside eating sweets. He is a large dog, and by virtue of that fact the resulting turd he left in Melissa's doorway was enormous. It took us some serious sucking-up and quite a bit of time to repair the relationship with the Newtons.

At home, I was routinely completing a lot of artwork to order, despite being an artist of the starving variety — if I'd been trying to make a living off it, I would be dead. I put pressure on myself to deliver works by certain time-frames that I knew I could barely meet, then gave myself grey hairs trying to. I knew how bad grey hairs looked among red ones (sorry — strawberry blonde) and I was too tight to want to dye my hair, so I was simply turning a fun hobby into an unhealthy obsession.

I had also written a book, which had recently been published. What would people think of it? Like this one it was an autobiography, exposing my flaws and failings as a front-line police officer (pre-AOS). Was it a little too self-effacing? It probably was, but I'm a big believer in 'warts and all'. If I were actually as cool as some of the people in the books I have read over the years, I wouldn't need to be self-effacing. I could just be that cool chick who did cool stuff all the time. If I'd lied and made myself out to be someone who never made mistakes, the people who knew me would expose me as a fraud. To me, that would be more troublesome than me beating myself up in print.

My new role on the AOS was a dream come true, but as the newbie and the only female, I was constantly analysing my performance, looking for mistakes. As in my early days in policing, whenever I carried out a physical task (such as getting into a scrap when trying to arrest someone), afterward I would assess my capabilities and look at how the manner in which I had handled myself would be perceived by my fellow police officers. Now, after every AOS job I would be considering whether I was tough enough to be a squad member. Was my decision-making good enough? Would I be accepted as part of the team, or would I always be 'on appro'?

Finally, during this 'who am I – where am I going?' assessment phase of my life, I thought about the other aspects of my day-to-day job. The most important part, really – the clients I dealt with: victims and complainants. They were no longer getting the best I could offer as an investigator. I was becoming disinterested in my work, and my mantra of 'Tell me everything . . . make your problems become mine . . . a problem shared is a problem halved' was becoming taxing and weary. I no longer wanted their problems; they could keep them.

The advice my relieving sergeant had recently given me began to gain traction. He had told me he thought I was trying to do too much. The book, the art, the AOS, being a detective, public speaking – I'd been doing the talk circuit for a bit, making about as good a living on it as I did with my artwork. It was great fun, however. I had started with Rotary groups and Lions clubs, then expanded to groups of little old ladies and Probus clubs. A great deal of fun, actually, because I got to talk about myself, my career and policing in general for an hour or so, then they would ply me with cakes and sandwiches and coffee.

Through all these different roles I was also a parent, carrying out a complicated juggling act with my time. My relieving sergeant said that with all my extra-curricular activities, he thought my core job was suffering. At the time, I denied it. I didn't like the criticism. I *could* do all this. And I could do it all well.

Or could I? I began, finally, to address the situation. *Change.* I needed change. Change was both good and necessary. A large part of my time in the CIB was spent working in child abuse, and I think I was running the risk of burning out. I was also feeling negative about policing generally. Before, I was able to talk with enthusiasm about the work I was doing, but now I knew I was boring people with my moaning about workloads, difficult clients and the like. Can you imagine sitting down to listen to someone talk with enthusiasm about their job, but instead getting: 'The world's stuffed. Everyone's stuffed. There are too many criminals. I hate criminals. They're stuffed. If I was the prime minister, I would . . .' While I never actually did this, I don't think it was too far off.

I was getting tired – I *was* spreading myself too thin. It took me a while to figure all this out, but I finally began to understand that I wasn't Wonder Woman after all. So, I decided to seek promotion in the uniform branch. You might think that would be the last thing I should aim for after all the moaning you've just read, but the job of a uniform sergeant involves a different style of policing. CIB work is demanding, all-consuming; it has a high workload (and hence much stress), and the arrests – which are few and far between – are usually for indictable matters, basically meaning that they end up in lengthy court cases some two years after the arrest. Uniform sergeant is about managing people. I wanted to manage people.

I applied for the first sergeant's job that came up. And I missed out. *Bugger*. In my usual style, I'd expected everything to happen because I wanted it to happen. Life doesn't always work out like that. (You probably knew this, but I'm a very slow learner.) I analysed the failure. The job was for sectional sergeant: shift work covering a 24-hour roster over a 10-week rotational period. In not getting the job, I wondered whether my cup was half-full or half-empty. I decided it was half-full – it was good that I didn't get it; I actually wasn't quite ready for shift work. My husband had supported my applying, but we knew the child-care would fall mainly to him as I would be working around the clock when I was on duty.

The next job that came up was for a community constable. Back into the blue uniform. Not quite the meteoric rise to the top I had hoped for, but perhaps the sideways shuffle was needed in order to get back into uniform and move forward. So I applied. And I got it. Whether I was ready or not, now I was moving. Goodbye, detective. Hello, community constable, here I come.

So, I had a new job. I was in a new station – which was a lot smaller than my other one. My job description was completely different. My hours had altered. But I was excited. My original uniform still fitted, which was nice, though parts of it were a little outdated. I was just entering my fourteenth year in policing, and things had obviously changed. Not the ugly pants, though. No, no, no. That particular piece of 'fashion' was going to withstand the test of time.

Why does the department make every policewoman wear pants that make her bottom look like a hippopotamus's? Do they think we don't know how bad they look? Do they not realise that we constantly catch reflections of ourselves in mirrors as we pass, and we groan every time? This is my plea: get us some new pants.

But aside from the pants, wearing the uniform felt good. When I first joined up, it had always made me feel great when I put it on, and I was satisfied to find that it still conjured up this same feeling. I took a pile of files with me to my new station – prosecution cases that were with the crown solicitor's office. Unfortunately, I couldn't just leave these behind. They still required additional follow-up, and all had trials pending. So there was to be no quick cut-off between the complexities and drain of CIB work and community work.

I was a little conscious of how my move would be regarded by my peers. Whereas before I had relished my role as detective, I was now back where I had started all those years ago. Vainly, I thought it might look like I hadn't actually gone anywhere in my 14 years. 'Who cares what people think,' I was consistently told by anyone I mentioned this to. Well, I did. Like it or not, I did care what people thought. So sue me. I'm vain.

I settled myself into my new police station. It was a small, independent station in a suburb of Palmerston North. As I sat behind my new desk, I found myself breathing an honest sigh of relief, and the makings of a smile crept onto my face. (I was the only one there, so I wasn't particularly concerned about looking loopy, smiling to myself.) I actually felt the physical sensation of weight coming off my shoulders. It was that clear. I knew I had done the right thing. I was no more and no less of a police officer than I had been; it mattered not whether I was wearing a uniform or not wearing a uniform, calling myself a detective or a constable, arresting someone for rape or overseeing the school crossing patrol. All that did matter now was my sanity and my happiness. I felt both saner and happier.

About two days in, while I was still trying to find places to put the multitude of police equipment and files I had collected over the years, I heard the phone ring. I was the only one on duty there that day, so answered it: 'Community station, Liz speaking.' The caller was a little old lady who was concerned about her neighbours' cat. They'd gone away for a week and had asked her to feed the cat, but then had left the cat locked inside and given her no key to get in. While she was telling me of this problem, I found myself smiling again: my first community policing problem. The smile was becoming habitual – the smile of a maniac, really. I loved it; I really loved this – this seemingly trivial worry that this lady had, which I needed to resolve.

I wondered why I hadn't made the shift to community policing earlier – it was less demanding, less stressful and, I think, earned more positive feedback from the public compared with what I had been doing before. Was I copping out with this new job? Hell no – I was recharging my batteries. They were flat and needed it. And trust me, the public would be happier with me here rather than in the CIB, where I would be silently but sulkily berating them for having the audacity to make a complaint at 3.58 p.m. on a Sunday when my knock-off time was 4 p.m.

I dealt with the little old lady's problem. Was the cat in danger of dying? No. Did this case warrant me breaking in and saving said cat? No. Would she be able to ring me if the situation changed in the next couple of days? Yes, of course she would. I hung up three minutes later, as satisfied with the result as I know the old lady was. I rang her back a few days later, just to make sure everything was A-okay. Yep – neighbours had returned. Cat had survived. Next case, please.

11
COMING OUT OF THE CLOSET

Just in case you accuse me of misleading you, I'm not about to tell you I'm gay. It's just that the next AOS job I'm going to talk about involved a house, a locked door, a man, and a closet. He could have been gay, though. I'm not sure; I didn't ask him. But he did come out of a closet and I watched him do it. He certainly wasn't gay as in 'happy' at that time, either.

I had been at my new community police station chugging through some CIB paperwork (still), when I heard a job concerning a firearm come up over the police radio. Two males and a female had been seen with some type of firearm as they were walking into the rear of a nearby property. I knew the property they had walked into well, through many previous dealings. As a safety precaution, a few officers had gone to get firearms and were then to take up cordon points nearby. I listened for a bit to see if there were any further developments or sightings of the trio, then heard the back door of the station swing open. Another of the community policing crew had turned up. I heard him rattling around somewhere within the station, so followed the noise until I found him.

He was getting a firearm out of a safe, so I joined him. I hadn't actually learnt how to access the safe up to that point, and joining him sure beat the ugly court file I was trying to whip into shape. As we roared down to the area in our marked patrol car, we kept listening to the radio for updates. There had been no further sightings. As we got closer we were given a cordon point, so moved in. From where we sat, we could see down the street to the address, so we crept back out of sight a bit – nothing like a large blue-and-white police car to blow your cover or your head off.

We'd been sitting there with eyeballs on the address for less than a minute when I heard the dulcet tones of my husband over the radio. At that time, he was acting AOS commander while the boss was on leave, and today he'd been listening to the job on the radio from the safety of his office. Once he had gathered the required amount of info, he announced to comms that he would now be running the job from his end as the incident controller. Seconds later, the AOS pager attached to my belt went off. Here we go.

I left my workmate at the cordon, and caught a ride back to the main station with one of the detectives at the scene. My heart rate was already going up in anticipation of the job. This family wasn't very nice, and the welcome mat certainly wasn't going to be rolled out to meet us when we arrived. I could guarantee that.

As we kitted up, my husband came in and started to organise sections. With one eye on the whiteboard that said who was to do what, I quickly climbed into my layers of gear, checking I had stunnies (stun grenades) aplenty, then got together with the section I was in. We discussed our strategies and then, with no time to spare, we headed off.

We stopped about 200 metres from the address, around the corner and out of sight, near where I had originally been on cordon. As soon as the door of the AOS truck rolled back, we piled out in a previously discussed order. Standing there waiting for the rest of the team, I tried to visualise what the address looked like. Visualisation is a good technique; it allows you to walk through, in your mind, the place you are going into – forewarned is forearmed. I wasn't always very flash at this, however – my visualising always tended to be over-imaginative, or wrong. When I actually went into the address, I would often struggle with what I was looking at. *This isn't right – there should be a door over here, not over there.* I would stand there arguing with myself for precious seconds about door and window positions.

Still down the street from our target, we checked each other's kit for security, and our own weapons for state of readiness, then lined up in our order of march. Over my shoulder was slung the 'karaoke' (loud hailer). I hated it. I know hate is a strong word, but this thing gave me nightmares.

In every call-out, the newbie gets the karaoke. So far, luckily, I had only had to use it once. There were jokes aplenty on my various AOS courses about it: 'We want to hear your great voice, and so does everyone else . . . make it loud and proud.' Despite the jokes, there was also lots of encouragement through your earpiece from the rest of the squad when you were actually doing it. It's a lonely job being the loudest one there – everyone else is in stealth mode, but you're singing from the rooftops, 'Here I am! In fact, here we all are! Come on out!' One of the squad is historically remembered as saying, 'Come out and no harm will come *towards* you.' He was sort of right. Another guy on my AOS course, during a scenario we were doing, turned the karaoke on too early and was heard discussing using the 'loud inhaler' with his offsider.

Today, the loud inhaler was safely attached to my kit. It banged around uncomfortably against my chest as I jogged forward into position; once there, at the front of the address, I unclipped it and sat it at my feet. All ready to go. I lifted my M4 up so that I had a view through the aim point at the front of the address, then waited for everyone else to get into their assigned positions. I took a few deep breaths to get my heart rate back down after the jog in.

Once all the squad had called in their readiness, the negotiators put a phone call in to the address. Engaged. They tried a couple more times without success, then I got the radio call I didn't really want: set up the karaoke. *Bugger.* I rolled my eyes – what about persevering? Try, try, and try again? *Bloody useless negotiators.*

By now, there was a fair mob of people in the area watching us from the safety of their homes, so the prospect of my voice reverberating off the neighbouring houses didn't fill me with joy. But an order was an order. I crouched down, pulled the dreaded loud thing out of its bag and turned it on. I tapped the microphone with a gloved finger. Nothing. Not even a squeak. The battery was dead flat.

I was secretly elated, but also saw that this wasn't a tremendously ideal situation. In our role, we did everything in our capabilities to invite the occupants to leave the house peacefully and without any resistance, so that we didn't have to use force against them. Having no means of talking to them cancelled out one of the options. But on the other hand, as anyone who knows me could tell you, my squeaky voice over a loud hailer was a very unpleasant experience. My squeaky voice *without* a loud hailer was a very unpleasant experience. Perhaps a flat battery saved the occupants of the house from a fate worse than death.

It's not an exact science as to who does the negotiating or voice-appealing. Sometimes a female negotiator is swapped for a male one simply because the subject might have just had a real barney with his wife, and the sound of another woman telling him what to do could put him over the edge. Regardless, today was not going to be my day.

As a precaution, we always carry more than one karaoke in to the cordon. Now, with my inability to make a decent noise – or indeed any noise – the squad members in position across the street were given the role. This was actually more suitable as they had a better line of sight to the address; they would be able to see what was happening as they gave their instructions. They set up their unit, and on 'Go!' a big, booming voice rang out.

'Occupant of 23 Nutt Street. This i . . . he . . . ice . . . a . . . me

. . . off . . . ders . . . sq . . .' Although their karaoke was going, it was operating like an out-of-range cellphone. There was a pause, and a clatter as the volume control was fiddled with, then they tried again: '. . . i . . . he . . . ice . . . a . . . me . . . off . . . ders . . . sq . . .'

I listened through my earpiece as they were told they would have to use voice only as the instructions were inaudible, and a few seconds later a booming, uninterrupted male voice rang out across the street. From my position right at the front corner of the address, I could see the front-door area of the target house. As the squad member appealed to the occupant to come out, there came shouting from inside the house. From where I was, I couldn't make out what they were saying. The instructions were again yelled out, and again I heard shouting from within. Someone was obviously home.

Having also seen movement in the front-door area of the house, the voice appealing immediately turned into a challenge: 'Put your hands in the air! Put your hands in the air!'

I could now see who they were challenging. A guy had come out the front door, holding something to his ear and at the same time looking up and down the street trying to figure out where the shouting was coming from. He began yelling back. 'What? What? I can't hear you!' He was called upon again to put his hands in the air and walk to the front gate, which he slowly began to do. As he walked, he continued to hold the object in his hand; I presumed it was a phone. The guy voice-appealing had also seen it, and yelled at him to put it down.

'I'm on the phone to the media!' he yelled back, while walking out onto the footpath with one hand up in the air and the other still holding the phone to his ear. *You what?* Talk about time, place and circumstances.

'Put the phone down!' he was told again, and after speaking a couple more words into it he lowered it to the ground in front of him, keeping his free hand up in the air. While a squad member behind me had their firearm on this guy, I kept mine trained on the house. Following instructions that were now issued by another squaddie further behind me, the guy walked past me; then I heard him being searched and secured, and the low, murmuring voices as they quizzed him. A short time later, we were told that another person might still be in the address, and that person had a warrant out for their arrest. They didn't want to hand themselves in.

The voice-appealing began again. The preferred, safest option is always to have everyone out of the house before we go storming in – for obvious reasons – but after the appealing had gone on for some time, no one ventured out. The wanted guy had obviously made a decision – he wasn't going to be coming out without a struggle.

An entry team was selected; and I was number four in it. Once our entry plan had been formulated, we all stacked up in order and made our way to the front of the house, where the offender had kindly left the door open. On 'Go!' we all swooped in, shouting out challenges that clearly identified us as police, and clearing the rooms as we went. As I reached each door, I would stop, heart pounding, then burst through issuing my challenge. Every time I didn't come across anyone my pulse would go up a beat – our target was here somewhere.

There was one room we hadn't yet searched. I had reached a closed door early on, so stood outside it waiting for the team to clear the rest of the open rooms. As well as being closed, it also had a keypad lock on it. Someone in the house didn't trust everyone else.

So, it was locked and we didn't have a key. Well, not the standard variety anyway. Two pieces of MOE (mode of entry) kit that we carried everywhere with us were the 'key' and the 'sledgie'. The key weighed about 5 kilos, and was a mini battering ram with two small handles uppermost and a flat head at one end. The sledgie was a sledgehammer. Simple, and effective. The people who carried the sledgies and the keys were called breachers. On this job, the mode of entry through the locked door was decided on: we would be going with the sledgie.

We lined up at the door and, on a nod, the breacher (who that day was G) swung the sledgie back and on the forward stroke punched the door open; within seconds, I leant forward and threw in a stun grenade. Once we'd heard the *bang!* we quickly entered the room, re-issuing our challenge as we did so.

Initially it appeared that no one was there, but while I had been clearing the main part of the room, G had had his firearm trained on a closed cupboard door. Once I was done, G and another squaddie, L, set themselves up for the cupboard. I stood behind them, waiting.

The door was popped open. Shirt, shirt, jacket, jacket, pair of legs, jacket, jacket. *Pair of legs?* L's black-gloved hand reached in and gave the legs a poke. Yep – they were definitely legs. The clothes were shoved to one side and the legs, along with the body they supported, were jerked out and pulled to the ground. I'm not sure who was more surprised at this point. The legs, or L.

The legs were attached to the body of the man who was wanted. He was held on the ground and searched, had cuffs put on him and then the remainder of the cupboard was cleared. Empty. I was left to watch him while the rest of the house was properly secured. As I stood over him where he lay on the floor, there was a stony silence. He was still breathing heavily, probably still a bit shell-shocked by the stunnie and his extraction from the closet. When he had regained his composure, he finally broke the silence. 'What's all this about?'

'Shut up,' I said.

That's what I love about the people we deal with in our job. They're all a quivering mess when you kick their door in and would bake you muffins and make you a nice cuppa if you told them to; then, when the moment of initial surprise has passed, they try to act all cool, calm and collected. *Why on earth are you here? What have I possibly done wrong? Firearm? What firearm? I was just hanging out in the cupboard in a locked room like I usually do, then you lot show up. What do you want? You've breached my human rights. I'm gonna call my lawyer. I'm gonna have your job.*

By the time the arrest team had come forward and led him out, he had a swagger in his step like he was 'the man'. His swagger was meant to show his neighbours that he was still a cool dude. So cool, in fact, that he didn't have to come out of the house when he was told to. He made no reference to the fact that, 10 minutes before, he had nearly crapped his pants in a wardrobe.

The next day I had a look at the front page of the local rag. Splashed across it was a blow-by-blow account of the arrest of the first guy out of the house, which had been heard over the phone by the reporter as it had 'unfolded'. I was immensely relieved that I hadn't had to karaoke him out, as one could only imagine what little gems of quotes I would have had displayed on that front page.

12

HOW TO STOP A CAR

In the AOS role, there isn't only the need to storm into someone's house to secure them — our offenders sometimes drive around in cars that have to be stopped. The tactics we use in stopping a car are thoroughly practised. And, I would have to say, that practising is the most fun you can have under the guise of actually working.

One job like this was a watch-and-wait game, which we spent an entire afternoon and evening on. The pager had gone off during the workday. I and the rest of the team turned up in the squad room and learnt of a known drug dealer who was apparently heading our way with a load of drugs in his car. To up the ante, he was also carrying a loaded pistol with him. If he came our way, we would be used to stop him.

We were all assigned different vehicles to be in, as each car had a designated role to play. I was to be bringing up the rear in the dog wagon, which seated only myself and the dog handler, with his dog in the back. We had some time to wait, of course, as drug dealers all run to their own time-frames. If a drug dealer had arranged to meet Jim at 3 p.m. at his place, it wouldn't be out of sorts for them to actually arrive at 10 p.m. We all changed our watches to druggie time — which effectively meant taking them off and calling home to say we wouldn't be back for tea, and quite possibly breakfast.

We began the waiting game at the central police station. A couple of coffees in, I thought about the wisdom of continued caffeine consumption. Once the coffee got 'moving', I'd have no hope of a quick toilet stop. I poured my remaining cup down the sink, then decided to make a trip to the ladies' to powder my nose before we had to go. Telling the boss I would be back in a moment and would keep my earpiece in, I slipped off.

I forgot that the boss was a prankster. A real funny one. As soon as I left the room, he walked around the rest of the squad telling them to ignore his next radio command. By this time I had secured myself in a cubicle and had begun to disrobe. Taking off the layers of Kevlar, fully laden outer vest and overalls, I put them all on the floor close to my feet. Of course, I had to leave the earpiece from the outer vest in my ear, which meant I was leaning forward on the loo with my head twisted to one side so that the earpiece, which was still attached to the outer vest lying on the floor, wasn't stretched too far.

Just as I committed myself to the action of peeing, I heard 'Go, go, go! We are go!' It was the boss's voice yelling in my ear. *That bastard*, I thought to myself. *It's a prank. Or is it? What if it isn't?* As doubt filled my mind, I quickly pulled all the layers back on, half did up zips and press studs, and after a cursory rinse of my hands under the tap raced out to the meal room. To see everyone sitting there. Drinking their coffee. And smiling. I grimaced at him; then, at my leisure, sorted out the rest of my half-secured kit.

An hour later, we finally got a heads-up saying our man had been seen heading our way. We all scurried down to our assigned vehicles, and at a decent clip headed off to intercept him. A short time later, we got to the point where we were going to do the vehicle stop and, after sitting stationary for about two minutes, we finally saw him peel past. We were on. The engine roared as the dog wagon accelerated. As with every job, my pulse rate immediately shot up, and I clutched my M4 in front of me with my right hand, holding on to the car door handle with my left.

ABOVE: With my siblings in the late 1970s. From left: Ruth, me, John, Becky and Sam.

BELOW: My first car – our family friend John Noakes painted the flying pig on the bonnet when I had gone out for the day. Funny that I went on to join the police . . .

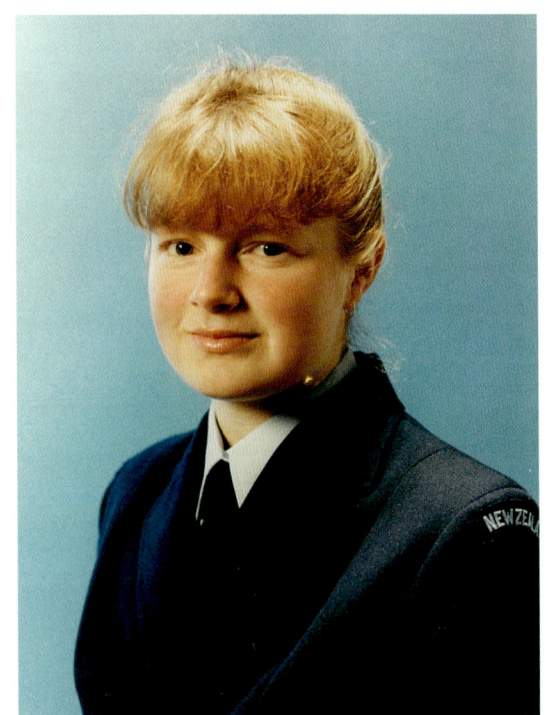

ABOVE LEFT: With my brother and sisters again. I'm on the bottom right with the spiky do. In hindsight, it didn't actually look that great.

ABOVE RIGHT AND BELOW: My Air Force days. I was about 18, looked about 13, and loved large fringes.

ABOVE LEFT: The belle of the ball at my 21st. I think I was dressed as a princess as the party had a medieval theme – complete with a codpiece competition (which a woman won).

ABOVE RIGHT: Getting on the wines at the best wedding of 2000 – mine! I don't recall much after this photo was taken but I've heard I had a great time.

BELOW: Posing with a local police shooting trophy in Palmerston North. I won it about three times – despite my dress sense.

ABOVE: With my gorgeous baby boy.

BELOW: The wonderful Newton family (our regular babysitters) with their cat, Squirt.

ABOVE: Hanging out with a tree – the perfect camo. *Photo by S. Burridge*

BELOW: With my good friend GB on our AOS qualifying course. I'm on the right, catching some sleep while standing up. *Photo by B. Harrison*

ABOVE: Arriving for the heli trip to Napier in 2009. *Photo by Mark Glentworth*

BELOW: I'm generally easy to pick out of a group of squaddies – I'm the vertically challenged one. *Photo by Mark Glentworth*

ABOVE: Doing my thing on AOS training days. *Photos by S. Burridge*

BELOW: Running the Dunedin half marathon with my sister Ruth. Her first, and I'm thinking my last. No need to push oneself unnecessarily . . . *Photo by Jonathon Simpson*

ABOVE: Hamming it up in my AOS kit. *Photos by S. Burridge*

BELOW: With my husband at a Christmas function in 2011. He's the one looking delighted with his catch. Me.

With our target in sight, the other two cars moved into position, leaving us to close in the rear. With a squealing of brakes and the sound of metal against metal, our target was stopped. As soon as the dog wagon halted, I pushed my door open and sprinted to the rear of our vehicle, behind cover. The dog handler reached the rear at the same time as me, and was already opening the back to get the dog out. Looking at its beady eyes, I could see the dog was keenly aware that something was happening.

Training the M4 on the left-hand side of the vehicle, I heard two loud explosions. Stunnies had been let off just in case the occupants had any doubt about our intentions. There was also a shattering noise as the heavily tinted glass on the side door of the target car was smashed, creating a hole through which a squad member could see anyone who might be in the back seat.

Behind me, I heard the sound of a truck idling – it sounded like it was less than half a metre from my heel. Always looking ahead at the target stops you getting hurt, so I wasn't able to have a peek at what was behind me until much later. It appeared that the truck had been directly behind us in the line of traffic when we stopped the drug dealer. When we sealed off the road with our stop, he had crept forward and stopped when we stopped. From where he was parked, he had a ringside view of the whole operation.

One by one, the occupants were brought out of the vehicle. To my surprise, one of them was on crutches. His legs were misshapen, bandy-shaped. As he hobbled toward me, I thought about how I was going to get him to kneel on the ground so we could secure him – his legs didn't look like they *could* actually bend at the knee. Then I made a mistake that I will never make again. I called him to me while aiming the M4 at him, then, when he got close enough, I *asked* him if he could kneel. In my defence, I have to say this feat looked physically impossible.

I should never have asked him; I should have told him. Let *him* figure out how he was going to do it. Of course, his reply was that he couldn't. So now I had a man on crutches to whom I had

HOW TO STOP A CAR

relinquished control, and a huge audience of the public who were now lining the streets around us, watching our every action. While I deliberated, the drug dealer started calling out to the people watching to take photos of what we were doing. We were picking on a poor guy with crutches. He forgot to mention that he was a drug dealer and that he carried guns.

Another squad member, R, stepped forward and pulled Mr Dealer down. To hell with public opinion – control was needed. Once the men were secured, they were handed over to waiting staff. The patrol cars that had forced the offenders' car off the road were disentangled from the side of it, the sound of ripping metal accompanying their separation. We all took ourselves out of public view; then, when the road was clear, climbed into available cars and headed back to central. I berated myself all the way back to the station for my one, seemingly small error of negotiating with the offender. Another lesson learnt.

13

AXEMAN

I was almost asleep when the phone began ringing one night. We had farewelled our friends about an hour previously, assigned the dinner leftovers to their various Tupperware containers, and fed and put away the guard dogs. We have more than just the pet one; unfortunately, the other one isn't fit to go out in public as it is extremely disobedient. And our dogs aren't actually guard dogs; calling them that just reassures me. It means I can sleep at night with my head under the pillow without a worry. Except when there's a possum hanging from the tree outside their kennel, like it often does at night. Their 'sod off you pest' bark is quite different from their 'intruder warning' bark, but still just as damn loud.

Anyway, there I was, waiting for the sweet oblivion of sleep to take me, when I was rudely interrupted. By the AOS phone and its annoying 'Austin Powers' theme song ringtone. My husband was acting as the officer in charge of the squad at the time, so any requests for AOS came via a phone call to him first, then he would hit the pagers for everyone else.

I was instantly awake and dug my husband in the ribs. Unlike me, he had already succumbed to dreamland. I lay there eavesdropping on his conversation, trying to get an assessment of whether this job was going to be a goer. Whether there was any likelihood that

I was going to get eight hours' sleep, rather than two. From what I could hear, it was heading down the two hours path.

I climbed out of bed and snuck downstairs out of earshot, then grabbed the house phone and dialled the number of our dinner-guests – the wonderful Newtons. I knew they would still be awake, and I also knew they'd be happy to come back and 'mind the baby' while we ran around in the night chasing people with guns. It wasn't going to be a problem if they couldn't come, however, as then I would have got my eight hours' sleep. After they had given me an ETAWDTSL (estimated time of arrival while driving at the speed limit), I crept back upstairs and got dressed. The negotiations were still going on by cellphone, discussions of things like the best safe arrival point for the team, and the legal power of entry that would be used. By the time it had all been arranged and the pager was letting everyone else know about how little sleep they would be getting, our child-care team had arrived. We were off.

I know we got sideways looks from some team members every time we both turned up during the night. The obvious question was always, Who's looking after your child? My usual joke was that he was down in the police yard in our car with a packet of chips and a bottle of coke.

We had been the last to arrive, despite our early heads-up from the phone call my husband had taken, so I climbed quickly into my kit, layer by layer, grabbing the M4 last, and scurried out to the waiting car. The town the job was at was a fast-paced 25-minute drive away, and we were heading initially to the closest police station to get a formal briefing.

We learnt that our target had been acting very peculiarly in the days leading up to this night. The local police had been to his house the day before as locals had seen him pacing around his property with an air rifle. No one had been threatened with it, but the police had been called as a precaution and they had taken it off him. On the evening of the call-out, he had apparently got even odder. This time, he had spoken to a neighbour about concerns that a gang was after him for drugs, but that they were mixing him up with his cousin. He told the neighbour that if the gang came, someone was going to die. He ended this with saying he would then head off and kill his cousin, whom he blamed for the gang's unwanted attention. Some time after this conversation, the neighbours heard two gunshots, which they believed came from his address. They again called the police, and those police in turn made the phone call to the AOS.

We split into our teams and were given the squad briefing, then clambered into vehicles and headed for our safe arrival point. My area of concern was at the rear of the address. The target's house was down a long drive, and there were neighbours stacked close by on all three sides. In a team of eight, we skulked our way down one of the rear neighbours' driveways, which took us directly behind where we needed to be. A large but brittle-looking composite fence greeted us, and right next to that was a dense, spiky hedge with fencing wire threaded through it. To get access to this guy's place, we would have to go over either one or the other of these barriers.

While I deliberated, the rest of the team continued to push through to their cordon positions. The moon was bright that night, adding to the glow from the surrounding street lights, and all I could see of the team was a mass of black silhouettes up ahead. I squinted in confusion, however, when they all stopped and one of the silhouettes started to get shorter. It looked like an invisible hammer was whacking him on the head, and he was disappearing into the earth. What was he doing? This was no time for fooling around.

I walked up to where they had stopped and could hear suppressed laughter, like that cartoon dog with the snigger like an outward gush of air accompanied by a squeak – Precious Pupp. The first squeaky laugh was joined by about three others, including mine. Q had stepped into some sort of mud pit. What it was doing in the backyard was anyone's guess, but it was working like quicksand on the fully laden squad member. No one was helping Q, who was steadily disappearing from sight, as we were all too busy laughing at him. Raising his firearm so it didn't also succumb, he somehow managed to extract himself and squelched his way off to a safer area of the garden – now with an additional camouflage of mud up to his mid thighs.

Distraction over, I returned to my hedge/fence choice. I was looking at them both, perplexed as to how I could do it, when S, another, larger, member of the team, motioned me to the hedge. Bugger – my last hedge experience on a job had been a disaster, and this one looked even thicker. I tried to tell S my thoughts but it was too late – he was already slithering his way through. He was about 60 kilos heavier than me, so nimbleness wasn't going to be safe ground for arguing the toss. In I went after him.

Lordy, lordy, I got stuck again. Bits of my kit snagged, and I knew I sounded like a herd of grumpy rogue elephants thrashing around trying to free themselves. Gritting my teeth, I briefly stopped thrashing to listen; apart from my racket, it was silent. I struggled again, and got through the prickly bits; now it was just the fencing wire. Somehow, by bending my leg and holding on to it just below the knee, I lifted it and tucked it over the top of the fence, ending up with my knee hooked over at waist height. Right, now we were cooking.

I pushed my M4 through, and leaning forward and breaking all the rules, tried to place the muzzle gently against a surface to brace myself, like a walking stick. *Crunch.* I'd connected with a nice white pebble garden. As well as being very noisy, it had the added risk factor of possibly lodging pebbles in the barrel. I tried reaching further out to brace it against something a bit safer. Concrete; that would do. Leaning well out, I placed the end of the muzzle on the concrete – making a nice loud clanking sound in the process. *God, when would this be over?*

Hopping my other leg forward, closer to the fence, I now lunged forward with my upper body and my front leg slipped fully over the fence, resulting in my crotch connecting with the top row of wire. *Oooohhhh.* Not very comfortable. Using speed as a last resort, I thrust myself completely over in one deafening move, freeing my genitals, leg and dignity at the same time. I crunched loudly onto the pebble garden below as I fell forward, catching myself on one knee and one hand, my M4 clattering onto the concrete in front. Pebble gardens are stupid. They are of no use. *White* pebble gardens are of even less use. They show up people dressed in black who are lying in them. They crunch loudly when stepped on. They don't grow plants but they do lodge themselves in gun barrels. They humiliate people. They should be banned.

I froze where I had landed, and listened. Nothing. A miracle.

S had already approached the side fence and was trying to get a view into the backyard. I came up behind him – nice and silently – and motioned that I would move forward. Where I was going would take me close to the front corner of the target's house. So far there were no lights on, and no signs of movement; the target was clearly hearing-impaired.

I gingerly approached a garden gate that took me even closer to the front corner and, once through, set myself up in what seemed to be a good pozzie. I was mindful of my helmet poking up above the low fence I was now crouched behind, but if our target came out the front I was well placed to intercept and deal with him.

I had been there for perhaps five minutes, listening through my earpiece to other members moving into position, when someone suddenly announced that the target had come out the back door with an axe. And a dog. A 'guard' dog no less. And I mean a *real* guard dog. As I caught my breath, I heard verbal challenges being shouted at our villain. 'Armed police! Put the axe down! Put the axe down! Armed police!'

Shit! An axe! This guy was about to get himself in a whole raft of trouble. I cringed in anticipation of what I would hear next – I truly believed it would be the sound of a 9-mm or .223 round. If someone is approaching you with an axe and they're not putting it down, your tactical options prior to using lethal force rapidly begin to diminish. The offender was forcing our hand.

As I listened to the AOS challenges, I also heard lots of loud crashing noises. What the hell were they doing back there? The crashes were accompanied by bangs, and more yelling. My eyes were still glued to the front of the house, and from what I was hearing, I was pretty happy that the target was creating the ruckus out the back and, at least for the next few minutes, I wasn't likely to be seeing any action from the front door.

I learnt later that the AOS member who had initially challenged our man had been behind a decent-sized fence. As the need to get closer to the man became a matter of urgency during the verbal challenges, he had elected to go through the fence as opposed to over it. The squaddies on the other side had done much the same thing. Hence the crashing and banging.

The villain began yelling back, challenging the AOS members to say who they were. Again they identified themselves, and told him to put the axe down. My breathing had quickened and my eyeballs – still glued to the front of the house in case someone else popped out from there – were drying out, they were so round. After what seemed like an eternity of yet more fences being broken and more yelling being done, it was finally announced through the earpieces that there was 'one in custody' – our axe-wielding target. The next information that drifted across the airwaves was that the dog was being secured, and finally that a team was ready to clear the house.

After all this information had been relayed through, it was announced that the target was being brought out – minus his axe. He was marched out the yard gate, past my 'sentry' point, and down the front of the address. He sauntered past me, a weedy, skinny wee white man who didn't look much taller than me, wearing his handcuffs with the air of someone who had 'chosen' to wear them. As soon as he hit the front gate, he became vocal and obnoxious. I could hear him blathering and complaining to the squad member who was posted to watch him, and I was almost surprised I didn't hear the sound of a size 9 boot being shoved into his mouth to shut him up.

The house was cleared. Apart from an air rifle no firearms were found, and the mystery of the other shots being fired wasn't ever solved.

14

DUCCAH, DUCCAH, DUCCAH

I love the unpredictability of policing: you never know what is going to happen from one shift to another. For example, on the morning that I was dithering about in front of the mirror in my bathroom, wondering whether I should put my hair up in something that resembled a bun with lots of hair pins in it, or leave it down in an easy-to-manage ponytail, I knew there was every chance the 'up' do would need to be ripped down in a hurry. I decided to tempt fate. Up it was. And it looked bloody spiffing, too.

I spent the morning carrying out mundane policing jobs that featured lots of paperwork, finding it pretty dull. But suddenly, something more exciting on the police radio made me prick up my ears. In a rural area near ours, two baddies had been on an aggravated robbery spree. They would rob one shop or service station, then drive off to the next town and rip off another one. They had been on the go for 24 hours straight and had passed through two police districts, but so far had got away with sod all except their liberty. They must have been holding out for the mother haul, but it wasn't to be their lucky day; it was to be ours.

Their most recent job had ended in a carjacking, and they had last been seen heading for our city. Every available patrol car was heading to their last-known location when one of our guys called up to say they had spotted the baddies' car in front of them. They were now following at a safe distance and were waiting for back-up to arrive, as they were unarmed.

In anticipation – *This definitely sounds like an AOS job*, I thought to myself – I headed to the main station and strolled nonchalantly toward the squad room. Hey there . . . I just happened to be in the area. What? A call-out? Well, how about that – I'm all ready to go as I just happen to be here already. Although the pager hadn't gone off, there was every chance it soon would. I was going to be early, for once.

While 'sauntering' around near the squad room, who should I find there? My husband, just about to hog a helicopter ride with another squaddie who'd been around. They were going to fly over as an emergency response unit. Without wishing to sound too pushy, I invited myself along. I was already there, after all.

My 'up' do nearly cost me my ride, however. How fast could I rip those hair pins out? Not very. First I had to find them among my bird's nest of hair, then extract them as quickly as I could – all so I could put my helmet on. Chunks of hair flew out as I ripped and pulled, and I heard pinging noises as the well-hidden pins flew across the squad-room floor and landed amongst others' kit. Sweating and panting with the exertion, I finally got them all out (minus one that I found later in the shower) and got the hair that hadn't been ripped out sorted into a more practical arrangement. A low ponytail.

As soon as we were kitted up, we located an available policeman complete with car and got a ride to the helicopter pad. As we drove, we listened to the updates. The offenders had realised the police car was following them so had turned up a dead-end road, obviously not knowing it was a dead end. The copper had followed them for some distance and then pulled back, knowing that he wasn't carrying a firearm and they now had nowhere to go. Out of sight around one of the last corners, however, and not known by him then, the baddies had actually abandoned their car and were legging it. A dog unit was also on the way over, along with another squad member, Q.

While we were still driving I managed to get a call in to the Newtons telling them what we were up to, and that we didn't know when we would be finished. As per normal, I was told to shut up and just go, as everything would be sorted. There was nothing I had to worry about except the job I was going to. As we pulled up at the helicopter pad, I thought about how cool this day was panning out. The helicopter had just been wheeled out of its hangar and was going through the start-up checks. We rolled out of the car and straight into the helicopter. I thought they only did that in the movies?

This is the coolest! Here I am, sitting in a helicopter, just about to go for a fly and catch some real bad baddies. Wow! I couldn't help but smile smugly to myself. The other squaddie, R, sat in the seat next to the pilot; he was to do comms. Next to me in the back seat was my husband. And then we were airborne. In my excitement, I hadn't given any thought to the fact it was a foul day weather-wise. It was raining, and very windy. To begin with, the small Squirrel helicopter we were in didn't seem to notice. Then we hit the Manawatu Gorge.

Anyone familiar with a gorge will know that it is a narrow body of water with large, steep hills surrounding it. The wind tends to whip around the hills – so, when we swung in over the top of them, we smacked into lots of airborne bumps and kinks. The Squirrel surged and dipped, climbed up then dropped to a terrifying extent. I glanced across at my better half, and the stupidity of us both being on this ride suddenly hit me.

If this thing crashed, we would create an orphan. I know that sounds melodramatic and you may think I'm daft, but it is a consideration one should always make when going out to deal with dangerous things. As best I could, I normally tried to keep myself separate from my husband when dealing with high-risk situations

– such as helicopter trips. Or bungee-jumping. Or eating uncooked chicken. Safeguard oneself from the 'what if' factor. But today, in my haste to get my hair pins out, I had not thought of this at all.

What if we did crash? Sure, our child would be well off financially, but he would be rather fucked emotionally. While still only six, I'm pretty sure he'd happily flag the money in favour of still having parents; spending the rest of his childhood being brought up by grandparents who farted and didn't even realise they were farting was another thing altogether. In fact, that was the sort of childhood baggage one would carry throughout one's formative years and was guaranteed to make therapists rich. (Just in case my in-laws and out-laws are now offended about the farting thing, I'm actually just kidding. I know that you do actually know when you're farting; you just choose not to comment. And that's okay.)

But now, here we were. Flying. Together. Risking it all. Thoroughly committed to the course of action we were on. Instead of asking the pilot to turn around, I accepted my fate – whatever it would turn out to be – and dug my fingernails into the tiny little seat and held on for dear life. One way or another, it would soon all be over. As we dropped away from the gorge, to my immense relief the wind gusts suddenly stopped, and another five minutes later we were at the area where the offenders had last been seen. We had survived.

The pilot hovered us around the baddies' now-abandoned car before following the road up into the hills, all eyes peeled for any sign of movement down below. I could see the dog handler, T, along with his AOS cover-man, Q, on the road below, but so far T's dog didn't seem to be tracking anything.

Next thing, R, on the comms in front, let us know that the dog was now indicating on the road below. The pilot banked around and took us down into a hover in a paddock, near where T now was with his 'indicating' dog. It was all systems go – or whatever the words are when you need to get out of a helicopter that's hovering, really quickly. Leaving poor old R in the heli with the comms, I piled out after my husband, who was leading the charge – ready to sprint across the paddock, over the fence, through the brambles and up onto the road where the baddies were hiding. Easy peasy.

As soon as I clambered off the skid and took the first two steps, though, I fell face-down in a swamp. A rather swampy swamp. It had all the swamp components, too. Black mud. Reeds. Water. Suction. I hauled myself up, trying to prevent the muzzle of my M4 becoming buried, and slurped my foot out of the mud. And immediately fell splat again. I was now on my hands and knees, thinking about the swirling rotors above me and my disappearing knees and boots below me. At least, with being this low there was no chance of losing my head in the rotating parts.

Feeling rather vulnerable with my arse in the air, one hand gripping my gun, which was hovering millimetres above the mud, and the other hand getting sucked into said mud, I managed to crawl forward baby-style, all the time watching my scrawny-arsed husband nimbly prancing his way through the marshes up ahead.

By the time I finally got a good footing and some decent forward motion, he was quite a way in front of me. Righting myself and attempting a burst of speed followed by a dash across a creek, I caught up to him at the barbed-wire fence. My breath was now rasping, my face red and blotchy from the effort, and my legs and hands a muddy, wet mess. I cleared the fence and the brambles, then scrambled up after my man. By the time I emerged onto the road he had reached T and the dog, who were only a few metres away from our exit point. T was standing over one offender, who was lying face-down on the roadside with his hands cuffed behind his back, and was motioning down the bank to where Q was trying to deal with the second offender. As soon as I reached T, I took over the guarding, allowing him and my husband to disappear into the brambles to help Q.

In the background throughout was the monotonous *duccah, duccah, duccah* of the helicopter rotors, hovering up above us. The noise was deafening and made communication difficult – either face to face or over the radio. By now, the offender on the ground had started to get his wits together and was rolling around a bit, trying to crane his head to see what was happening with his fellow robber in the bush below. A boot placed gently between his shoulders had him looking the other way again; and a minute later, number two villain was hauled out of the thorns to join his mate.

I then noticed the dog handler's hands – they were dripping with blood and seemed to have holes in them. I looked at the robbers, who appeared fine, and asked T what had happened. He told me how his brand spanking new, just-out-of-its-wrapper police dog had been so overcome with excitement at the imminent capture of two fugitives that he'd bitten his boss. Twice. T said he was going to class it as his dog's first bite. Fair enough, too. I'm sure his dog manual didn't specify whose blood it had to be.

The patrol cars that had been on cordon were now called forward and the four of us walked the two robbers up the road to meet them, walking past the abandoned vehicle and the police car that had stopped at the corner behind them. After a recap about our actions on locating them and the fact that they had been told their rights, they were handed over to the cordon staff. With the helicopter still hovering in the paddock next to us, my husband motioned me over and told me we would be returning in it. *Bugger*.

We trudged back through another bog and into the waiting heli. R was still sitting in the hot seat, not a scrap of dirt on him but with a slightly peeved look on his face. I knew he would have been cursing. He was never happy to miss out on any action, least of all helping to capture armed villains at gunpoint. Though, looking at this job in its entirety, my role hadn't actually involved anything other than contributing to a pile of washing, as I was now covered in bog peat *and* sweat.

But would I have preferred to stay at my desk and complete the paperwork that really needed doing that day – or chosen to look fear in the face by pulling all my hair pins out in a hurry (risking unsightly hair loss), then flying in a *very* scary contraption and falling in a bog, getting my very clean boots and overalls all dirty and in need of a good overnight soak in Napisan? There's no choice. Napisan every time. It's the price I pay.

15

COWBOYS AND BADDIES

When I was a kid growing up, I often dreamed of living in the era of the American cowboy. I used to love watching old cowboy movies, with their old-world towns and the characters that lived in them. Their streets were always wide and dusty – unless it rained, but it seemed to only ever rain at night when the baddies were riding in to kick some good guys' butt. The rain helped set the theme for the spooky 'here come the baddies' music.

These towns would be complete with a saloon – the hub of social activity for the blokes (and the ladies of ill repute who serviced the blokes) – a general store that sold everything from nails to flour, and the sheriff's place, which also had a jail. Outside every store or building was a hitching rail over which you flung your horse's 12-foot-long leather reins when you arrived. Why they never came undone always baffled me, as when I was eight and tried flinging my 6-foot-long binder-twine reins over our farm fence in an attempt to hitch my fat, 12-hand brown horse called Pedro to it, he always ended up buggering off up the paddock without me.

My desire to live in this era was also fuelled by watching the Milkybar Kid on his big white horse. You might remember that ad – it was a big white horse, he was a little blond kid, and they were marketing Milkybars (which I love). Pedro never helped me with my imagination. The Milkybar Kid's horse used to rear up at the end of the ad, and the Milkybar Kid would wave at the camera. The closest Pedro ever got to rearing was when he shot his head up fast from eating grass because he thought some hay was coming his way. If I happened to be on board at the time, from where I was sitting it was almost a rearing movement.

In the movies, I loved watching the cowboys battling against the Indians (probably not a very politically correct thing to say today). I loved the chases on horseback, the dust, the baked beans around the campfire, the card games in the saloon, the outlying rocky mountains – but mostly the sheriff. I wanted to be a sheriff when I got big. His town was his domain, and woe betide anyone who messed up the natural order of things. He (it was never a she, but that never slowed my imagination) knew about all the local ratbags, and as soon as they crossed the line he would sort them out.

But as time went by and I grew up, I realised that I didn't really want to be a sheriff. They worked alone; all the time. I was a pack creature. Safety in numbers, that was me. I still wanted to catch the baddies, but I also wanted to be part of a big bunch that was catching the baddies.

This extremely long chapter intro leads me via a somewhat roundabout route to small-town cops. Small-town cops in New Zealand are to be respected. Their towns are remote, back-up being anywhere from 30 minutes to three hours away, and as a result they are often ingenious, tenacious, and certainly not lacking in initiative. I score pretty low in all those areas, which wouldn't have helped my childhood sheriffdom quest. But these guys are like old-time sheriffs.

A busy town cop knows that if they start something that might lead to a confrontation, back-up is moments away. Small-town cops need to employ different means. They may have to back off and rethink their strategy. It might mean returning the next day when the baddie is sober, and arresting them then. It might be they spend 40 minutes negotiating with the person before they are able to talk them round to putting the handcuffs on themselves. Whatever the method, the decision they make could mean the difference between losing the fight or living to fight another day.

One day, as a fully fledged big-town cop, I came across one such town and one such sheriff during an AOS job. The sheriff wasn't a gung-ho horse rider, but he also wasn't one to turn a blind eye. It turned out that some ex-locals had come back to his town after spreading their mischief around other parts of the country for a few months, and on their return had begun helping themselves to other people's stuff. Some of that stuff was guns. Our sheriff had run across the villains fresh from their burglary, figured out pretty quickly what they had done – and what they now had – but did his maths. There were four of them, and one of him. Instead of launching in and grabbing them straight away, he called the cavalry. Since they weren't around, he got the Palmy AOS instead. This sheriff used his initiative. He was going to use us to get the baddies out of bed bloody early and create a wonderful element of surprise, combined with cops en masse. So, at an ungodly hour, we headed over to the town.

I felt awful on the way over. Our designated driver, G, was fast and furious, driving the patrol car like he'd just stolen it. My head lolled around on my shoulders where I sat in the back seat, and I wished I could just vomit and get it over with. Rolling out of the car when we arrived, the two tonnes of kit I was wearing pressed into my stomach cavity, causing an involuntary retch into the gutter. It was very un-cowboy-like. I gathered my stomach contents together, willing them to stay put, then headed over to join the rest of the mob for the briefing.

Our lawless customers were spread out over a number of addresses. Depending on how we went on the first one, we would then split up and check the others. I knew one of the targets, by reputation only, from a homicide inquiry I had worked on in the previous year. He was painted as a real arsehole, and from what I knew of him, if I could have chosen a preferred format for a first-time meeting, this would have been it.

We arrived at the first address and fanned out into our spots to wait for some action. As we waited, the negotiators put in their first call to the address. It was a success, of sorts, in that it was answered – but the person who answered it told them to get stuffed, and hung up. They rang again, and again it was answered. Then, quite unexpectedly, people started coming out. I was in the meet-and-greet party (we make quite a reception team), so I assisted in lining them up and handcuffing them as they popped out in their pyjamas.

Then I heard a racket. 'What the fuck do you think you're fucking doing, you fucking pigs? You've got the wrong fucking house . . .' Blah, blah, blah. It was the arsehole. And he sounded just like I'd imagined he would sound.

He was walking out the way the others had, but he was very unhappy about it. He wasn't, apparently, a morning person; but to be fair, I don't think he was a lunch or an evening person, either. Whatever time we'd chosen, I think we were going to get the same reception.

He was challenged by squaddies to put his hands in the air as he stormed out, but it was doubtful whether he could have heard any of the instructions over the sound of his own voice. He continued to rant and rave, telling them to get fucked a lot. He carried on out through the front gate, where I was standing guard over one of the other occupants; then, when he was out and clear of the gateway, he was told to get down onto the ground. 'Get fucked,' he instructed his instructors.

A couple of masses of black-clad, focused fury sailed past me, and Mr Morning Glory was detained and in handcuffs faster than you could say, 'the Milkybar Kid rocks'. Situation under control. Once everyone was suitably sorted so that they weren't going to cause any problems, we formed an entry team and cleared the house.

During the search we located a couple of firearms, which made the whole early-morning thing more than worthwhile. And the local sheriff lived to ride another day. Go, the sheriff!

16

STOP THE CAR, I FORGOT THE GUN

Policing entails many responsibilities, and some sure put you in good stead for joining the AOS. Ultimately, policing brings a new challenge every day. One day from my early career stands out in particular, a day when I had a very important role with a VIP.

It would have been just like any other day, if I hadn't forgotten to bring a gun. I then added to the occasion by also doing a petrol drive-off. All while on duty – but not just any duty. On this entirely forgettable day, I was supposed to be the élite personal protection officer (PPO) for the Prime Minister. A cut above. The best of the best. Prepared for any situation . . .

This happened just before I joined the AOS, when I was still a detective in the CIB. At the time, I was a trained PPO, or bullet-catcher. My husband had always thought it was a bit of a joke for me to try to stop any bullets from hitting someone I was protecting. I would need to leap in the air at exactly the right moment, as I was almost always at least half a head shorter than the VIPs. I loved the role, though. Again, it was an interesting distraction from my day job, as the AOS would later become.

The task I had received was simply to 'look after' the Prime

Minister. She (it was then a she) usually travelled with her own Diplomatic Protection Squad (DPS) member, but when she came to our area, we boosted the numbers. That day, the team comprised myself, a workmate who was interested in joining our élite team (whom I'll call John), and an already serving PPO, name of B.

To simplify things, B had asked us to uplift a firearm for him from the police station, then pick him up on our way. He lived out of town and it seemed a perfectly reasonable request. As we drove out to get B, John and I chatted about this, that and the other. Along the way we passed a steaming carcass by the side of the road. I glanced briefly in my rear-view mirror, hoping it wasn't a dog which had just been hit, but as time was of the essence and we had to be at our destination shortly, I had to keep going. The carcass wasn't moving, it was clear of the road and, from the amount of steam issuing from it that cold winter's morning, one would hazard a guess that its insides were now its outsides, and it wasn't going to be responding to any kiss of life.

We arrived at B's house, and after the standard greetings, set off again. About two minutes down the road, however, I discovered that our fuel was quite low. We had a two-hour drive to get to where the Prime Minister was flying to, so I thought it might be a good idea to fill up. B directed me to the closest petrol station, and I pulled in. While I stood holding the petrol nozzle, I discussed with John and B who was going to pay. Each police car has a fuel card, so I handed said card over to them to deal with. At the same time B asked where his firearm was, as he wanted to take the opportunity to put it on while we were stopped. I looked at John, and a feeling of dread immediately came over me. I had forgotten the firearm.

I was *so* embarrassed. Here I was, trying to give John the appearance of knowing what I was doing, and I had blown it by being forgetful. We discussed how to go about getting a firearm without driving half an hour back in the direction we had come from; then came up with the idea of getting a firearm from the local police station. B immediately set about calling them up on the radio. But they were busy – checking out a steaming carcass by the side of the road, which a member of the public had phoned in to say they'd hit about 20 minutes previously. And they had taken the firearms to finish it off.

We tried in vain to get on the radio to tell them what we knew about the state of the steaming carcass and the fact that a firearm wasn't going to be of much use, but comms was so busy giving directions and instructions to the local police about how to find the roadkill that we couldn't be heard. When we finally did manage to make contact, we quickly established that we wouldn't be able to borrow any shooters because they weren't likely to be back inside of 30 minutes, which would make us late for our pick-up.

Fortunately we had brought with us a spare long arm (M4) – which wasn't ideal, but manageable, so we gave this to John. John had brought his own sidearm, so we relieved him of this and it now became B's. After all this was sorted, I finished refuelling while both B and John disappeared into the shop, emerging a short time later with assorted drinks and snacks. We would cope with this situation. That's what policing was all about – overcoming obstacles and adapting when faced with adversity. No worries, mate.

Finally we set off again, laughing at ourselves cheerfully and knowing things couldn't get worse. Then B's phone rang. His 'Yeah, yeah. Oh,' answers were slow and dragged-out, and said while staring at me with a smug grin on his face. 'Thanks, mate.' He ended the call, then looked at me. Again, I felt dread. *What now?*

'Did you pay for the petrol?' he asked me.

'No – I was refuelling, remember!' I wracked my brains to try to remember who'd had the fuel card last. *Nope. It definitely wasn't me. I think.* In the excitement of forgetting the firearm, and talking about the dead sheep, we had got so distracted that we'd forgotten the fundamentals of paying for petrol.

At that time, petrol prices had begun to go up a lot and petrol stations were more and more often becoming victims of drive-offs, the most commonly used method of saving a buck or 20. 'Well,'

I said to myself in consolation for our error, 'we've been told to try and think of ways to tighten the purse-strings. I'm sure police management are going to be delighted with this very inventive cost-saving initiative.'

Comms had been trying to call 'the silver Commodore who had just refuelled' on the air for about 10 minutes, but it appeared we had our radio too low and never heard the call. The local police officer, one of those who had gone to slaughter the already slaughtered sheep, put two and two together and, obviously knowing about our poor morning performance to date, rang B. After a round of us all blaming each other, B got on his phone again and called the cop back. Like a well-oiled machine, he greased up a request to have the local cop pay our debt.

We did manage to get to our destination that day, we did manage to protect the Prime Minister without incident, and we even managed to drive home. But it didn't quite end there. The following Monday morning, perhaps two days after our debacle of a day, the detective sergeant in my office came storming over to me, waving a bit of paper. I had only just arrived at work and hadn't yet managed to regale everyone with my 'forgot my gun then did a petrol drive-off' story, so he completely ruined any chance of my getting a giggle by barking at us, 'Who the hell was driving the silver Commodore over the weekend?'

'Me,' I replied, immediately on guard and with a nervous smile playing on my lips.

'Well, there's a theft file for a petrol drive-off you did.'

'Don't worry about it. It's all sorted,' I said by way of simple explanation, but was cut down with: 'No it's not!' Apparently, the cop who'd been asked to pay hadn't done it. I was now a fugitive from the law – for theft of petrol.

Now, it's only recently that I've wised up to some things in life. One is this. Even if you make the stupidest mistake in the world, if you get the opportunity to tell the story yourself, in your own words and in your own time, to your own audience, you can look a little less stupid. That audience is yours. You can embellish your version, leave the really incriminating stuff out and repackage what was a stupid moment in time as a humour-filled event that your audience is lucky to hear about. No, not lucky – privileged. But this is all destroyed if someone announces your punchline first, and does it with the intention of making you look like the twit you are. It loses the funny factor. And, let's face it, no amount of retelling the lead-up is going to make it funny now.

'Sort it out now,' he told my now red face, as he stormed off. I kept blushing and at first tried to explain, but ended up just snatching up a phone book and the file, and skulking over to the phone to 'sort it out'.

I dialled the petrol station in the little town, and introduced myself as the idiot from the police who had done the drive-off. I was greeted by silence, then the lady saying 'What?' So I explained again. I also gave my name – which wasn't a good thing because I had rung the wrong petrol station. 'Try our other one down the road,' she laughingly told me. So I did, and this time kept it short, sharp and unfunny. How many petrol stations does one small town actually need?

I swallowed my pride, I paid, then I swore when I hung up – because, of course, it hadn't actually been me that had had the fuel card.

17
YOUNG LIVES CUT SHORT

One of the main differences between day-to-day policing and AOS jobs is the personal contact. You see the bad side of humanity in both jobs, but when you're on an AOS case you move in, control the situation and move out, generally leaving someone else to deal with the parties involved. With jobs like a homicide investigation, a police officer has much more contact with the people involved, and often for a much longer period of time. While it depends on your role, you typically become much more connected to victims and their families, and even though violent crimes are never easy to forget, they affect you much more when you are on the case day in and day out.

Murder is the most horrific of crimes. Its occurrence often appears random. The people surrounding the victim's life are left shell-shocked and devastated, and that one victim becomes tens of victims through the way their friends and families are left behind to deal with the tragedy. In 2005, I was honoured to work alongside a very special family on one such tragic homicide in Wanganui. By this time, I had already worked on a number of homicides while in the CIB. In each one, I took on a different role. For the Wanganui homicide, which was named Operation (Op) Somme, I was given the role of victim liaison officer.

The victim was a young woman called Tania. She had been found one morning in January, the morning after her twentieth birthday, beaten to death and floating in the Whanganui River. It wasn't known how long she had been there for.

By the time Op Somme occurred, my husband was on two months' leave and therefore able to cope with child-care, which gave me the opportunity to travel to Wanganui to work alongside the homicide team that had just been set up. I arrived one day in, and on my arrival, was introduced to the detective senior sergeant who was running the inquiry – Mike Oxnam. He was an imposing figure, and looked a hell of a lot like Shrek. I wondered immediately if I would ever have the opportunity to tell him this. I didn't have to – within the first couple of days, he set me the challenge of trying to guess what his nickname was. 'Shrek,' I answered, without a thought.

'Who told you that?' he asked. He wouldn't believe that no one had. A bit later, I met the second-in-charge of the inquiry. I thought it appropriate that he should have a suitable 2-I/C name. So Donkey it was. On that first day, Detective Senior Sergeant Oxnam, or Ox as everyone mostly called him (Shrek was still a newish nickname, and not really very complimentary toward someone you didn't know that well), took me to meet Tania's family.

They were a lovely, very ordinary family, trying to come to terms with the most extraordinary grief of losing their cherished daughter, and sister, Tania. The fact that she had celebrated her twentieth birthday the night of her death made the waste of her short life even harder to comprehend.

There was a raft of extended family and friends with them at their house. I especially felt for Tania's parents, Naelene and Garry. Not only were they coping with their own grief, but they were also trying to comfort their other children and their daughter's friends. Everyone was suffering. I stayed long enough to introduce myself, and Ox explained to Naelene and Garry the role that the police inquiry would play. I left them my details for any questions, and returned to the station.

Meeting family early in an inquiry such as this one motivates you even more to catch a killer. Seeing their suffering, hearing their endless questions of *how, why, where, who* – none of which we were able to answer at that time – made me want to help them more than ever. We couldn't bring their daughter back, but we could do everything in our capabilities to find out who took her life. And that's what Ox assured them we would do.

Working with Ox was a very positive experience in my CIB career. He was a man you wanted to do well for. He described how, when he kicked off a homicide inquiry, the first thing he did was surround himself with positive people. People who wanted to do well. People who gave it their all. I understood that. And I understood how dedicated the people who worked for him were – his teams were often hand-picked, and were described by others as 'Ox's travelling roadshow'. He didn't know me from a bar of soap; I was his wild card – Palmy's finest. Actually, I'd been the only one who was available, so I'd have to work hard to earn the reputation.

As the days went on, I met often with Naelene and Garry. Through them, I began to learn about their daughter. Through Tania's friends, also, I found out what sort of girl she was. No one ever wants to speak ill of the dead, and it is often hard to coax details from people about what a person was really like. We needed a 'warts and all' account, as it could provide a motive. It might also lead to a person that Tania knew, whom we needed to talk to. In time, we got this picture – and the thing was that Tania, even warts and all, sounded like a really good sort; the type of person a lot of people liked. Her death had truly left a huge chasm in everyone's lives. Some days when I went around, Naelene and Garry were having a good day; sometimes they were having a bad day. The more I knew about their daughter, the more empathy I felt with them about their loss.

As the inquiry progressed, a picture began to emerge of a particular associate she'd had. I'm not going to tell you the name, for the following reason. The thing with homicide inquiries is that, after the media have followed it in the initial days, through the different phases of the inquiry and then through a court case, and the offender is known and has been named, often no one remembers the victim's name — just the offender's. This suspect was a male with a violent criminal history and an extremely volatile temper, and had been around Tania the night she had disappeared. He was well known to Wanganui police.

The details of Tania's last night began to become clearer over the weeks of the inquiry. Effectively, Tania had said 'no' to him. His lies and deceitful cover-up after he had murdered her — washing clothes and items relating to her death — laid testimony to the sort of character he was: one that was better off inside a prison than out.

He was interviewed by a colleague of mine from Palmerston North, C. During C's interview with the offender, what emerged was a man who was hung up on his sexuality. He thought he was god's gift to women. To his way of thinking, he could get any woman he wanted. It made the idea of him killing someone for spurning his advances somewhat more likely.

After months of meticulous inquiry work and file preparation, carefully led by Ox, the man was charged with Tania's murder and put before the courts. At his trial, one could be forgiven for thinking we had the wrong guy. His usual number-one cut had grown to a tidy crop of hair; his abundance of 'hate' tattoos were masked by neat clothing. He was well dressed and presented, and looked almost respectable. Clues to his real character were, however, exposed through his defence. His girlfriend at the time of the murder was offered up by him as being the likely suspect; she was said to have the motive and opportunity. However, an intelligent jury saw through his continued deceit, and found him guilty.

At his sentencing he flagged any pretence, and came as he usually was — tattooed, with a shaven head, and a look of hate on his face. He subsequently received the mandatory life imprisonment sentence. I was happy to see Tania's family again at the sentencing. No one ever fully recovers from losing a loved one through murder, but seeing them again more than a year after their daughter had been taken from them, and watching their strength and courage as they sat through the sentencing, I appreciated how, sometimes, the gift of time can help people cope that little bit better. You should always remember that when you view a homicide through the media, you get only a small sample of what those left behind will have to live through for the rest of their lives. It's not just offenders who get life sentences.

18

DRUGS, DRUGGIES AND RUGBY TACKLES

The team you work with in the AOS are a dependable group – after all, your lives are in each other's hands. And this doesn't just apply to the AOS: in policing, you need to know – and generally do – that the cops you work with every day have got your back. It's important that you are a close-knit team, as any situation can potentially explode. But sometimes, even during stressful day-to-day jobs, we can create a social occasion.

In the CIB, every once in a while we would have a warrants day. These consisted of the gathering together of previously unexecuted search warrants, a large group of staff, a free barbecue at lunchtime, and the promise of at least one lock-up for each staff member. As the cherry on the top, you didn't have to spend a long time investigating anything before you got to go and have fun. Warrants days gave us a great break from the usual office cases, which always involved protracted investigations.

We had already done a couple of warrants this day and found relatively piddly amounts of cannabis, when I was handed the next folder. It told me that the occupant of the address was selling large amounts of cannabis from home. Without very high expectations about what we would find, I briefed the team I was with, delegating particular roles (such as who was looking after exhibits, and who was taking the other occupants); then our convoy of six set off.

I was with fellow CIB member Pat. He was also an ex-boyfriend, but as we had both moved on some years previously, both procreated, and neither of us were hung up on issues arising from working with an ex, the conversation was as it would be with any other workmate – inane jokes, idle gossip and regular smart comments about each other's weight.

We pulled up a little short of the address and got out, walking quickly up the driveway. As soon as I had the rear section in sight, I saw a guy standing there – our drug dealer. He was just about to go into a caravan that was parked halfway between the house and the back fence of the property, but as he glanced over his left shoulder and saw us he clearly thought better of it, spun around to his right and bolted toward the back fence.

'Stop! Police search warrant!' I yelled as Pat and I ran through the front gate and to the back of the yard. The drug dealer had now reached the large back fence and was clambering over it. It looked about 2 metres high, was made of corrugated iron, and seemed to have no purchase on the side we were just about to try to get over. As I reached it first, I gritted my teeth and leapt. The SRBA (stab-resistant body armour) I was wearing made me teeter on the top, until I got more forward momentum and toppled over. With a grunt I landed on the grassy bank on the other side, and looked up to see the retreating form of the druggie.

At this time I had begun to do a bit of training for the AOS, so had done a few runs – but these were long, slow plods, not sprints. I wasn't sure how successful a foot chase now was going to be. As I set off, I heard a thud as Pat hit the fence behind me. Standing at about 185 cm and well over 100 kilos, I cringed at the thought he was going to topple the entire fence and still not make it through. A '*Haaaaaah*' sound as all the breath left his lungs and he hit the ground on my side showed that he had indeed made it.

I then heard a second thud as another team member, Bugsy, hit the fence. Weighing in at about the same as Pat but minus the height, I pictured him hitting the fence like a bird smacking into a window it hadn't seen. My imagination served me right; his legs were scrabbling unsuccessfully trying to get a footing, and he finally gave up and ran back out the address and round the side.

Meanwhile, Pat and I were now in hot pursuit of our druggie. As he ran, I saw his hands moving around in front of his body. I feared the worst – that he was armed – but then saw things getting flung over fences – drugs, most likely. About 200 metres into our 'race' he began slowing down, enabling me to gain on him. His hands were still hidden and he refused to show them, so while still running and fumbling to get my baton out, I yelled at him to get his hands in the air. This stalled things for a few seconds, allowing Pat to catch up; when he arrived, we hit the druggie simultaneously, rugby-tackling him to the ground.

He fell face-down with Pat on his head area and me on his mid-section, with me trying to drag his hands out from underneath his body. I kept yelling at him to show his hands, but he kept refusing. I shoved the pointy end of my baton between his upper arm and his body and tried to prise one arm out, without success. Finally, I warned him that if he didn't bring his hands out, he would be hit. When he still didn't, I gave him a couple of taps. I think he had both hands locked together under his body as I was trying to drag them out, but finally he loosened his grip enough that I was able to get his hands free. Putting handcuffs on him, we rolled him over to see what he had been concealing. Nothing. He just didn't want to be arrested.

We pulled him to his feet and marched him down the road to a waiting car. Pat searched him and found $400 cash in one of his pockets. It was all in neat, crisp $20 bills – coincidentally, $20 was the going rate for a cannabis tinnie. While we were having running practice with this guy, the rest of the team had continued searching his address. They found a further $4000 in cash, and about 17 cannabis tinnies.

As the arresting officer, I became the file-holder. As this guy had had many previous dealing offences he was kept in custody pending a trial for the drugs charges, which he had decided to defend (he was innocent, of course), and during this time I began the monotonous task of preparing the file for court. There was, however, a relatively new custody procedure available that was used for some of those who were remanded for a long time. It was called electronic bail, and it placed the detainee on house arrest where they wore an ankle bracelet around the clock. Mr Druggie was fortunate enough that he was granted this luxury, so while I slogged over the file he hung out back at his house.

He was, however, not yet quite reformed. While waiting for his court date to roll around he must have got very bored, so he continued where he had left off and kept selling drugs from his home. Getting some info about this, a UC (undercover) buy was arranged, and Mr Druggie helpfully sold a few tinnies to – unbeknownst to him – a police officer.

Chucked before the court again, and sensing a losing battle, Mr Druggie pleaded guilty to this charge and was sentenced to jail. He was now without his ankle bracelet, instead having to spend a few years in the big house – but he still didn't plead guilty to my case. Although we are sometimes allowed to use evidence of similar crimes committed *after* the offence with which a person is charged, in this case I wasn't. When my case went to trial, however, despite pleading his innocence and saying that we had set him up by timing our arrival exactly when he'd just received a load of drugs (I'm not sure how this was intended to work toward his innocence), a jury found him guilty of possessing cannabis for supply. He is now languishing for a further four or so years in jail.

19

MIXING IT UP IN THE FARMING COMMUNITY

While some AOS jobs end up being reported in the media, not all are eventful or deserving of such fanfare. There are, literally, hundreds of jobs done by squads around the country that the general public never knows about because things run smoothly – or, more likely, the media never catch a whiff of them. Whatever the job, though, we always go in at 100 per cent.

This particular AOS job didn't sound too complicated when we were briefed. It was an assist job really – we were to be the hired guns. Members of our local CIB needed to carry out a warrant on a house out of town where the occupant was reported to have firearms. He had also committed a kidnapping, and there was talk of drugs being in the mix as well. The theory is always that it's better to go in too heavy than too light, so our pagers had been set off.

We were all trucked out to the location, then sat around while the squad bosses tried to nut out an approach. Generally, night-time is a friend of the AOS. The colour of our clothing hides us easily; we can melt into the night's shadows, and as long as we aren't stomping about like elephants, we can arrive undiscovered at the target address, surround it, then watch unobserved for as long as we need to before inviting ourselves in.

Daytime is a different kettle of fish. We have to try not to be seen by using cover and concealment, hiding a bit more on our way in or enlisting the element of surprise – like perhaps roaring up a driveway and leaping out at the last moment: 'Surprise! We're here!' This was going to be a daylight job as our targets were where we needed them right now, and it was unsafe to wait any longer.

Shortly after arriving, we were called together and the plan was presented to us. Those at the rear would have to skulk across paddocks using whatever cover they could find, and the guys who got the front were just going to roar in. I got the rear. We set off at a quick trot across lush, green pastures with me in the lead. Immediately I reached a creek that I dithered over. Getting stuck in mud and water unburdened is one problem; getting stuck carrying firearms and heavy kit is quite another as it makes it more difficult to pull yourself out. I quickly scoured the 10 metres of creek either side of where we'd hit for something to form a bridge; but by the time I had found a Lizzy-size plank to use, the rest of the squad had waded past me, apparently unconcerned. Biting the bullet, I followed suit.

My boot squelched into the mud, and I had to lunge forward before I went with it. One obstacle down, though. The next was a fence, which the squad all helped each other over and through. I always found these difficult. Most of the blokes' crotches would clear a fence when they had a foot planted either side; mine would land smack on the middle of it.

Once clear of the fence, we had arrived at the rear of the house, so I set myself up behind a slight rise in a hill and surveyed the scene. The little farmhouse in front of me looked pretty rough. The actual house was surrounded by a few small sheds and garages, with lots of dense foliage and unkempt gardens. They all afforded good cover, but made it a little difficult to see. I had no doors on my side that I could see, which would make my wait pretty quiet.

Around me the rest of the squad members were settling into position, calling in their locations through the earpiece. Around one side of the house and facing the rear was a set of French doors. From what the rest of the team could see, that would be the most likely entry and exit point for both our offender and, if need be, us.

The call finally went up that everyone was in position, and a phone call was made to the house. I rustled around uncomfortably, waiting for the call to be answered. From where I sat, I could neither hear the phone ringing nor see anyone moving inside. Finally, after what seemed like an age, the PNT advised that contact had been made with a male. He was coming out of the French doors.

As quietly as a lamb, this man walked out the front of the house and clear of the property, finally getting handcuffed on the road outside. It was all over, just like that. With the intended target now secure, along with a few others I was called around the front of the house to a new spot, while an entry team formed up to go in. Again, I sat and waited.

As they made entry, I listened to them shouting their challenge to anyone unfortunate enough to be still inside, then watched curtains twitching in windows, and the Glocks' associated torchlight scanning the darkened rooms inside. Nope. No one home.

Once the team was happy the house was clear, we were called over to a waiting CIB car. I and three others were to get rid of our kit, leaving us in our overalls, and become the search party. Grumbling a bit to myself, as who wants to search grubby old farmhouses, I shed my layers and our newly appointed search team streamed inside.

As soon as I stepped in through the French doors that led into the lounge, directly to my left I saw an open rubbish bag that was chock full of smelly rubbish. I don't care what anyone says, the sight of an open and smelly rubbish bag in someone's lounge is right up there with animal do-do inside a house. Gross.

But the fact that my attention was drawn to it was perhaps the reason I saw what was uppermost in it: a plastic bag full of cannabis.

The occupant must have thrown his stash in there as he exited the house, in the hope that we wouldn't have the stomach to search their garbage. But regrettably for us, in our job that's exactly what we end up having to do. At least this find justified it.

Putting the cannabis to the side I continued with my search, finding various amounts of cannabis and drug utensils along the way. When one of the bedroom doors was pushed open, the stench of dog and cat urine and faeces greeted us. The dreaded animal do-do had been found. Closing the door must have been how the people in this house had dealt with their problem.

Undeterred, we continued to search, returning triumphantly to the station at the end of the day with our haul. The occupant was later convicted for the drugs and the kidnapping, making the entire operation a well-justified though slightly stinky success. Sadly, that wasn't the first search I'd ever had to conduct of a gross and smelly house, and I'm pretty certain it won't be my last. One of the many joys of policing.

20

OPERATION PEE

I just *know* that on the day when I have had the least sleep, I'm likely to get the longest call-out. Or even two call-outs. That's how Murphy's Law operates. I had just been on a school camp. Owing to the fact that the kids were only little, it consisted of a tent city in the school's yard, and was only for one night. But one night was all I could handle. Being kept awake until 4 a.m. by giggling and talking in the next-door tent, then getting woken again at 5.30 a.m. by more giggling and talking – and that was just the other parents – meant that I was a grumpy mother helping at next morning's breakfast. All through the night I had also endured hearing the relentless pattering of little feet, as the kids ran from tent to tent. I'd had three stink bombs let off in my tent (by the teachers, not the kids) and my tent had been let down twice (teachers again). All these shenanigans had caused me to mutter some very naughty words out loud – and, since the tent fabric wasn't noise-proof, in the presence of some very impressionable ears.

My lack of sleep was capped off by my previous foolhardy offer to take a carload of the little monsters out for a day trip. By then everyone was quite tired and intolerant, with lots of tears spilled for seemingly small problems. Some of the kids cried, too. I was thankful to get home.

That night I collapsed into bed at 7.30 p.m. I could barely keep my eyes open and the bed felt a hundred times more comfortable than the tent arrangements I had endured the night before. I was snoring within seconds of climbing in. Then, at 12.30 a.m. I was ripped from slumber by the AOS pager. The shrill beeping confused the hell out of me. Where was I? What on earth was going on? Who was beeping?

I slowly figured it out and squinted at the page. 111 – the code for 'Get to the squad room now.' It was a call-out, all right. My husband and I looked at each other. Unusually, the Newtons weren't available this night so we had to choose who was to go. As luck would have it, I'd had to set the alarm for 5.30 a.m. the next morning anyway; we had an AOS observation job jacked up that I was going to do. The chances were that this call-out could take me right up to it, and if my husband went now and wasn't back by 5.30, it would affect me getting to my prearranged job. I won the toss – or lost, depending on how you rate sleep and AOS jobs.

I ran around getting my things together and drove like the clappers into work. While climbing into my kit, I learnt that we were heading to a nearby small town where a drunk local man had decided to commit suicide. He had last been seen wandering off into town carrying a .303 rifle and a box of ammo. He was serious.

I was to be in the first section, and the rest of my carload was already ready to leave. Shoving my earpiece into my ear, I joined them and we set off; but by the time we arrived at the town, the situation had changed slightly. The guy had now returned to his house without the firearm and his partner had left, leaving him stomping around with a small child asleep in one of the bedrooms.

We viewed the maps and plans of the house and street, adapted the teams' placement to incorporate the lay of the land, then moved forward to our target's house. I led my team to the front of the address – no mean feat, as I had no idea which house it was. Once I had got to what I hoped was the correct house, I propped myself against a tall fence and kept my eyes glued on the address while the rest of the team assembled behind me. I was then called forward, right to the front corner of the address, by U, who was waiting across the road, hidden behind a fence and some bushes.

There was no phone in the house. In fact, unhelpfully, the only phone was with the partner who was at the police station, so any voice contact would have to be made via karaoke. Once we were all in position, T was given instructions to start voice-appealing from the rear of the address. On cue, he began.

His clear voice rang out across the quiet town, but inside the house there was no sign of movement or any indication whatsoever that he had been heard. No curtains twitched, no lights turned on, no voices yelled back. T continued relentlessly: 'Occupants of 3 Nutt Street. This is the Palmerston North Police Armed Offenders Squad. Your house is surrounded. Come out the front door of your house with nothing in your hands, where you will receive further instructions.' On and on T went, repeating the same words with minor variations such as chucking the guy's name in, or telling him to turn a light on if for some reason he couldn't move. But still no sign of anyone.

C helped out by hurling a few rocks onto the roof to get the occupant's attention. Except that C had the forearms of a Russian tree-stump puller, and many of the missiles he was throwing were completely clearing the roof of the target house and hitting the side of the neighbour's house. He was told to throw a bit softer. A bit more like a girl, perhaps?

Even with the continued yelling and the chucking of heavy rocks onto the roof, nothing changed in the house; we were still greeted by silence. Except from the locals. It was a Friday night, and partway through his voice-appealing, T was interrupted by an annoyed, drunk and obnoxious local man. He had staggered his way to T's cordon position to tell T to shut up as he was annoying his sister with his loud voice. Being the good big brother that he was, this man had come out to 'sort us out'. As T relayed this information to us via his radio, I could hear the drunk still sounding off at him in the background. Finally, T told us he would be arresting the drunk for obstruction as, despite the best advice given by T, the man would neither shut up nor sod off. As luck would have it, this drunk was also on home detention, meaning that he was in breach by having moved off his property in the first place. He was whisked away in a waiting local patrol car to be dealt with later.

T continued appealing for some time longer. A few more drunk people popped into our cordon area, yelling helpful things at us like 'Pig shit!' They would hover around the edge of the cordon for a bit, giving further supportive verbal encouragement to us; then the snuggly and comforting beer blanket they would be wearing would slip down off their shoulders a bit and they would stagger off again, too cold to offer any more advice.

After what seemed like an age – having not been fortified by alcohol, my teeth were now also chattering – a decision was made to quietly go into the house and see where our man was. While I stayed put, an entry team filed quietly past me and into the front yard of the address. I watched the windows for signs of movement on their approach, but saw nothing. The team reached the front deck area and I could hear the soft but audible thumping of their boots on the deck as they made their way across to the entrance.

Their shadows loomed outside the door for a few moments longer, then they all silently disappeared inside. I listened intently for signs of a struggle from within, but for the longest time could hear absolutely nothing. Then, from the front lounge area, came the unmistakable thump of a body. Describing it afterward, F said that as they entered the lounge they could see a shape on the couch. En masse, they all crowded around the shape and saw it was the snoring, comatose form of our male target. F had the time to quietly secure his firearm, line himself up with a set of handcuffs at the offender's exposed but limp wrist, which was draped across his stomach, and before the guy was even awake, he had been dragged off the couch and onto the floor with one handcuff on. By the time he came to, he was in custody. He was confused to begin with, then pretty grumpy after he'd recovered from his shock. Miraculously, the little child in the house slept through the entire affair in a rear bedroom.

A wander down the road to the last place the man had been seen with the firearm turned up the described .303 and a box of live ammo. It was hidden in the nearby school's playground.

As soon as we had both offender and weaponry in our possession, we drove back to our station. I looked at the time – 4.30 a.m. There was no point in going home as I would have to get up half an hour after hitting the sack, so instead I decided to do some paperwork, have an extremely long shower, and sort out my kit for the day's planned job.

By 6.30 a.m. I was feeling surprisingly awake. I had defrosted in the shower – which was about half an hour long – drunk a cup of strong coffee, and downed a couple of nutritious muesli bars for breakfast. The boss had also shown up, and I'd badgered him to buy me a small, famous but not quite so nutritious burger to wrap up my meal. Thus fuelled, I set off with a team of fellow AOS members to our next job, which was located, not to put too fine a point on it, somewhere in the wop-wops.

We were dumped at our entrance point, which was a small track. In the quiet light of the morning we filed silently down it, alert to any other signs of life as we went. As much as I was trying to keep an eye on what was around me, I was also concentrating hard on staying upright. The terrain we were covering was uneven, and the 25 kilos I was carrying in my kit and on my back kept throwing me off balance when I tilted to one side to go past a bush. A number of times I stumbled and began lurching off at an angle, trying to get my feet to catch up with my upper body before it toppled. Straightening up after one such episode, I glanced at my team-mate, K, who was behind me. He just shook his head at me, as if to say 'What is the AOS coming to?'

When we got within cooee of our intended set-up area, two of the team crept stealthily forward while the remainder of us took up a cordon in case there was anyone inside and they got flushed out. If they did, we would pop up and say gidday.

As soon as we got the all-clear, we moved into the area we were to be operating in. One by one we set ourselves up in a comfortable but hidden spot, then began to wait. And wait. And wait. I quickly found out that I'm not the best person for this type of job, as I'm impatient and also a fidget. Within the first 30 minutes I had already consumed a quarter of the food I'd brought in.

In the quiet bush setting, propped up in my camo gear and thoroughly bored, I analysed my remaining supplies and discovered that food can be broken down into two groups. One is the 'noisy' group, and the other is the 'smelly' group. Noisy food is further broken down into 'quiet' or 'loud'. Quiet food is usually soft, like a sandwich with something like jam in it. It could also include a banana – although these cross over into the smelly food group, which can be detected by the average nose from quite some distance away. A cold sausage is quiet food and, as long as it's not submerged in a casserole is also not smelly, but a crinkly plastic bag full of rice crackers is definitely loud food. Today I had noisy food – two bites of crunchy fresh carrot was all I would allow myself, as the racket I made chewing meant that I couldn't hear anything but me. I saw that K, who was nearby, had an apple (they're in the noisy *and* smelly group, depending on the variety); from where I sat I could hear him bite into it but not chew, so I allowed myself the luxury of eating my own apple, pausing every few munches to listen. I then drank one cup of coffee, and counted all the birds I could see.

With my eyes rolling back into my head with the boredom, I experimented with how much more acute my hearing was when I opened my mouth, then closed it, then opened it again. I stretched my legs out in front of me and tested how far I could flex my toes with my combat boots on. If I took my glove off, how quickly could I put it on again? Were both my gloves exactly the same, or were they different? I was bored shitless. I poured myself another cup of coffee. Then another. I was allowed; it was decaffeinated. I ate a lollipop, carefully tucking the wrapper back into my kit; then I ate another lollipop. They were a clever food, as they could be either in the noisy or the quiet group depending on whether you were a cruncher or a sucker. (I'm a cruncher.)

Sitting there, as the mind-numbing hours rolled by, I began to get cold. The trouble with not moving is that your circulation slows, and the longer I sat still the colder I got. I would have to put on another layer. I carefully pulled my wet-weather pants out of my bag and smoothed them out. It's at moments like this when I learn just how many everyday items we use incorporate Velcro. The whole sides of these pants were Velcroed, and pulling them on could involve a tremendous amount of noise. Very slowly and very carefully, I peeled the seams apart; then, wriggling around where I sat, I slowly pulled the pants on. I was also wearing knee pads that I had to take off, and these were held on with Velcro, too. Care paid off as I achieved my task, despite the noises seeming to rip and tear into the silence all around me. Once I was rugged up and concealed fully again, I fell back against the tree I was under, exhausted with my mammoth effort.

All too soon, however, I needed to go to the toilet. The decaffeinated coffees had made their way through. If I'd just been wearing my overalls this wouldn't have been a problem, as I had modified them by adding a special extra zipper round the crotch. Now, with my wet-weather pants over the top of them, there would have to be some sort of plan. (But at least this exercise was going to consume a decent whack of time.)

I informed my offsider what I was planning; he wished me luck and I set off to pee. I quietly made my way to a suitable spot, then carried out a check to ensure I couldn't be seen by criminals or fellow squaddies alike. I was good to go. Operation Pee was about to enter phase one.

Over everything else I wore, I had on a giant camouflage poncho. For this occasion where privacy was a must, it served as my own private toilet cubicle. Crouching down with legs bent at odd angles, I pulled pants down, overalls aside and began my mission. The relief was immediate, but as I peed I began to become concerned that I couldn't hear anything landing on the leafy forest floor. I wasn't getting any warm sensations down my leg or anything, so I knew it wasn't ending up in my overalls. So where was all the pee going?

When I'd finished phase one, I checked. The ground below my 'tent' was remarkably dry, as were my overalls. I was confused. It hadn't evaporated, had it?

Pulling the poncho aside to get better light, I saw where it was. A giant puddle was suspended in the waterproof lining of my overtrousers and hovering precariously in the air. As the sun glinted off its shiny surface, I grew alarmed. Any sudden movement would result in the puddle heading off down my leg. It would be all over; I would be drenched in urine. What the hell was I going to do with it? I still had another 10 hours to go, and I didn't want to smell of my own urine for that entire time.

As I stared at it, I carried out a tactical assessment. If I ripped the Velcro sides of the trousers apart, I might be able to pour it out without it touching any part of me. But it would be noisy. Very noisy.

To hell with noise, I thought. *I have dignity to preserve.* Sitting down while taking care not to tip the puddle, I gingerly began to peel the sides of the over-trousers apart for the second time that morning. After every couple of rips, I stopped and listened for the sound of approaching bad guys. Thankfully, I heard no one. I ripped as quietly as I could until the suspended puddle could be tilted groundward and emptied from the pants. Once this was done, I began pulling the wet over-trousers completely off. I wanted to set fire to them, so annoyed was I. But phase two was nearly complete.

I was not to escape without a little more drama, however. With one leg still to disengage, I suddenly heard loud voices. I froze, utilising my newfound technique of opening my mouth to hear better (making me look like a halfwit but furnishing me with super-hearing). It was a man and a woman talking, and they sounded like they were across the other side of our location. My offsider K quietly called the team on that side and asked if they could see anything. S reported back that he had thought it was us talking and had just been about to tell us to shut up. He then said it seemed like the couple might be about to walk over to his location, possibly forcing him to confront them.

It appeared that these people we could hear were following another track that ran behind us all. We had no idea if they were friend or foe, but if they saw S they would blow our cover and he would have to react. I took advantage of their loud talking to rip my over-trousers completely off, then stood up. My Glock, which I'd undone from the thigh holster for Operation Pee, dangled uselessly at my side, so with further cursing and gnashing of teeth I did it up again, and quietly moved forward to K's position, smelly wet trousers tucked under my arm.

Heart pounding, I sidled up to K and both of us strained our eyes to catch any approaching movement. S updated us from the other side with the direction the voices were moving in. From where I was positioned it seemed they were skirting right around the edges of where we were, probably as far as 50 metres back. By now they would have to make a sharp left to find us. As anxious moments ticked by, the voices began receding. K and I silently held our position for another 10 minutes, then S reported that the couple was no longer near him. When it became safe to move again, I turned to K. 'I peed on myself,' I confessed.

He looked at me first in confusion, then gave me the same look he'd given me earlier when I'd nearly fallen over. *What on earth is the AOS coming to?*

Suffice it to say, Operation Pee was the most exciting part of my day. The team who took over from us were briefed with the helpful advice to not pee on themselves. No baddies turned up on their shift, either that day or the following day.

The learning exercise I took away from that day was valuable:

don't drink coffee of any sort on a stake-out. And to prevent further hassle, I'm currently working on a modified pair of wet-weather trousers. They have a large inner-leg zipper and absolutely no Velcro.

21
CRIMINALS WITH JOBS

On each AOS job you attend, you are presented with a new set of skills to learn. Just how *do* you sneak up on a place in daylight when the occupant has a full visual on you for the last 3 kilometres of your approach? As I've said before, getting to a remote farming location unnoticed in daylight is next to impossible. The ingenious manner we carried out this next job, however, helped considerably. In fact, I think we took incognito to a whole new level.

It was quite hot weather, which made kitting up rather unpleasant. As soon as we left the relative coolness of the squad room, sweat began pouring off me. We all hoped we wouldn't have to be waiting around for too long. Today's job was to intercept a cache of firearms that our info suggested was just about to be moved and disseminated among some gangs. The weapons had been stored by a third party at a remote farm that had a total of one road in, so our mission was to secure the house quickly, getting in place with an element of surprise to allow a team in to search safely.

Our bosses had spent a bit of time putting together a plan, which, ultimately, was quite simple. Our entry and arrival would be made in a small box-truck, nothing like the police vehicles we would normally roll up in. While one of us drove, the rest of us would be in the back, and as soon as we got the word we would roll the back up, leap out and say 'Howdy.'

We rehearsed getting out of our borrowed truck smoothly a few times. I and another squaddie, U, were assigned to roll the door up then jump down, each to one side of the truck, and take up a forward-facing position, covering the rest of the team as they followed us out.

When we were happy that we had it sorted, Y, who was our driver, got into the cab and the rest of us climbed in the back of our new tactical-assault vehicle. Y was a laid-back, quiet fella who didn't look too out of place in the cab of the truck. He had a shirt over the top of his armour, and I would challenge anyone to pick him out of a line-up as a trained and lethal machine. Today he looked like Bob the truckie.

We trundled off down the road, the 10 of us in the back packed in like sardines. There was a tiny window that looked forward over the cab, affording one lucky soul a view, but the rest of us rolled around with the country road's bumps and dips, trying to hold on to our lunch. U and I were parked up right at the rear next to the roller door, as we would be getting out first.

As we got closer, Y gave us the two-minute-warning call. U and I crouched with our hands on the bottom of the roller, waiting to rip it up. The 30-second call was given, and in my mind I visualised myself pulling the door up smoothly, hopping off the back, running to the front and providing cover.

Our front-window man called out that we were now turning into the driveway, and that Y was waving gidday at two people standing in front of the target house. The two just stood there, watching our arrival with interest. Apparently neither of them looked like they were about to make a run for it; they probably thought the truck was there to drop off an item of furniture. One of the people was our young, foolish target – a kid who was about to find out he had bitten off more than he could chew by offering to work with gangs.

The other person, we were to learn, was the kid's employer – a farmer who had no idea what sort of employee he had.

On 'Go!,' U and I yanked the door up and we both jumped down. As I ran forward I saw the kid and his boss, so immediately began yelling at them to put their hands in the air. My M4 was held in front of me, leading the charge. U was also yelling at them from his side of the truck, so I shut up and allowed him to bark the orders alone. From the looks on their faces, the two of them seemed to be taken by surprise.

Both targets put their hands in the air; then, when told to get on their knees, their faces registered, 'But it's wet on the ground.' They got yelled at some more, and slowly lowered themselves down. Their hands were stretched out on each side of their bodies, palms uppermost to reveal they were holding nothing. Once they were under control, I was left to watch them while an entry team stacked up on the little farmhouse's front doorsteps. On 'Go!', a crashing sound was heard as they smashed in the pane of glass on the front door, and all disappeared inside.

I looked at the two lying on the ground in front of me. The farmer had inclined his head toward his worker with an inquisitive look on his face. I think the look said, 'What the *hell* have you been doing?' The young fella just rolled his eyes in response, which I read as 'I have no idea.' But he most certainly did have an idea. He knew *exactly* why we were there. Now, after his initial surprised reaction, he began cockily looking around the place and at us with interest. Either he was good at hiding his nerves or he was just an overconfident little twit.

After a short time the team re-emerged from the house and I heard one of the guys calling for medical help. Just what had they been doing inside? It turned out that when Q had gone through the broken door to clear the house, his forearm had connected with a shard of glass that had been left sticking out, leaving a deep gash. As he was getting his breath back inside, he registered that his arm was a bit wet. He looked down and saw a large amount of blood seeping through his sleeve. S was with him, so immediately applied pressure; then Q was whisked away to hospital and stitched up.

Once the house was cleared, we did a search of the outer sheds, which took some time. A number of live rounds of ammo were located, but the firearms had gone. We were too late – perhaps our trusty truck should have been something a bit faster.

The job completed, we all piled back into the waiting AOS truck that had now come forward. The little box-truck was driven off by Y, its former cargo having successfully created a good element of surprise, though unfortunately without the desired result. When we got back to the station we debriefed, and analysed the success of what we'd done. All in all it had worked well, the method of arrival getting us right up to where we needed to be, but it was disappointing not to get what we were looking for.

Before we were able to de-kit, in came a new job. This was to be our third in 24 hours. We had been given a new possible location for the firearms. The address was in town, and our tactic was to drive close to it, all bail out (this time we weren't in the box-truck) and hit the address en masse. The difference between the two jobs was huge. The first had been a planned and precise exercise, but with this one, because of the way we had received the information, we had to roll with it quickly and adapt as we went. Although we were each assigned a role, there had to be more versatility in the way we were about to operate. As Q was still getting stitched up he was going to miss this one, so we would also be one man down.

We arrived near our target and, co-ordinating our approach from each end of the street, on 'Go go go!' we all poured out of our vehicles, over the front fence, across the lawn and into the house. To both our and the occupants' surprise, we found a house packed with people. It seemed that the people who lived there had been entertaining a few friends.

They were all neatly contained in one room of the house, and as the squaddies burst into this room compliant hands shot up in the air everywhere. While most of us were out at work earning a living that day, this lot were congregating at a mate's house on a weekday afternoon to smoke up in lieu of contributing to society. Well, in a way I guess they were contributing – they were keeping me in a job.

They were held in the room by a couple of squad members as the rest of us continued through, the individual body searches being left until we had finished clearing the house. As seemed to be happening more and more on AOS jobs, I got shoved up a roof cavity. I was finding that I was regularly getting thrust under houses, too, although with all the equipment I wore I could have argued that I was as wide as any other member of the team.

Aside from spiders, the roof cavity was clear. By now we had cleared the entire house and also a rear garage. Apart from the group inside, there was no one home. The garage had an old car in it with drug utensils strewn around, showing signs that someone had been using methamphetamine there. The knowledge that along with missing firearms were meth-type drugs didn't sit well with me at all.

As the only female officer present, I was then sent back inside and given the task of searching the female occupants. My other least favourite job. One produced a stash of cannabis from her pocket, which I handed over to the inquiry team who by now had come forward.

Once all the remaining occupants were sorted and had been led out to the rest of the inquiry team staff, we stayed to assist with a closer search. In the backyard, well hidden, we again found live ammo. But once more, we didn't get the firearms.

Q turned up at this point – I think so he could show off his new war wound. He was fully kitted up again, but his injured limb had the sleeve removed from the elbow, displaying what he had been up to earlier in the day. The cut arm bore a large, clear sticky plaster, a few black ends of stitches rubbing up against it, and lots of blood sloshing around underneath. He was clearly there for the sympathy vote. My face wrinkled in distaste at the blood. Although

Q had ended up with rather a lot of stitches in his forearm, he was determined to not miss any action; however, I bet that once all the painkiller injections had worn off, he wasn't going to be so brave.

The firearms we were looking for never did show up. I often think about the ones we miss when doing jobs like this. They are likely to be used in robberies, gang shootings, stand-overs and the like, and I always cringe at the thought of the poor sod who'll be at the business end of them. At least that day, it wasn't us.

22

PALMERSTON NORTH'S MOST WANTED

When you're looking for someone or something, one of the best ways of finding them or it is to advertise in the media. This can be as unsubtle as 'Have you seen this man/woman/car?', or something a little more elaborate. My husband once, ingeniously, suggested to a butcher who'd had some meat packs stolen that he put a notice up in his shop window with the surveillance image of the thief, saying that the lucky person featured in the picture was the winner of a competition. The not-so-clever thief fell for it, and when she turned up to uplift her prize, the police were called and she was locked up.

The media provide one of the most useful tools we can use in policing, as they reach a greater audience than we could ever hope to. Although you might get a few false leads, with lots of similar-looking people brought to your attention, often you end up with your target — be it a car, a person or some other thing.

Recently we had been looking for two guys who had been on the run together for a long time. One of them had been running for eight months; he was wanted for wounding with intent to cause grievous bodily harm. This man had assisted in kicking a guy to within an inch of his life, and had split straight after he was committed to trial on charges relating to the crime. The other was wanted for robbery offences. The robber was also a former prison escapee, and there was no doubt that if either one of the two had got a sniff of us in their vicinity, they would be running. We also knew that both of them had firearms, hence our involvement in an AOS capacity.

These targets' staunch-looking mugs had appeared in the local rag some months previously without any immediate result; then, after a period of quiet when we received no more information about them at all, we were suddenly given an update. They had both been seen in town, and both had been trying to get more firearms so they could shoot at an opposing mob – for reasons known only to themselves.

The house where they were rumoured to be was in a busy area of town, and it was just after lunch-time. Many of the squad had been involved in the last (successful) pursuit of one of these targets a couple of years before, and so were pretty keyed-up about what to expect this day. My involvement in that previous chase had been when I was pre-AOS; I'd been part of a CIB cordon, ending up transporting him to the police station when he was finally captured.

Now fully involved in the squad for this search, I was given the front of the address with a few of the others in the team. Parking in a side street, on 'Go!' we jogged around the corner to the house. I was in front and, as I rounded the corner, I saw a man standing on the footpath outside. It wasn't the target and he hadn't seen us, so I motioned this to the team leader, C, then ducked between a few cars as I continued weaving my way forward. As we got closer, the guy turned around and walked back down the drive. It had been as if he was waiting for someone.

By now, the noise of traffic rushing past was joined by the sound of a helicopter hovering overhead. The detective organising the search had employed it in case these guys did run. As I reached the front corner of the house, a team member across the road, Z, began yelling at someone I couldn't see. It was the same guy who had come out the front, and he was now on the far side of the house from me, still standing in the driveway.

On Z's continued shouts, the guy sauntered out to the front corner and, following directions, wandered past me and into the receptive arms of C, who was positioned behind me. A few moments later, two little kiddies and an older woman walked out the front door of the house. As I had my M4 trained on the door they came out of, I immediately dropped the muzzle away from them when I saw how old they were, and allowed Z to tell them where to go. Again, like the guy, they walked past me and to C.

As I watched and waited, I heard talk that there were more people in a rear flat. One by one, they were negotiated out of the front of the house and onto the street by the AOS team members placed at the back. Still the helicopter hovered.

One particularly cocky young woman strolled out with her hands hovering up above her head and then lowered them, in defiance of the instructions given. I barked at her to get her hands in the air and they shot up again, this time staying in place. She was followed by Super White Fella – ignoring the yells because he was so tough he could do what he wanted. From behind me, I heard C give him a verbal burst, then there was a bit of light scuffling as C took him into custody.

By the time the house had emptied, it was evident that the targets had slipped off before we'd got there. I joined an entry team to clear the front house to make sure, and we stacked up at the door. On 'Go!', away we went. The house was definitely empty, although some ammo was found. We then received advice that the vacant place next door could be another possibility. Finding a partially open window, I was hoisted through into the house. I covered the room in front of me with my firearm pointing at an open passageway as the rest of the team piled in behind me. Again we cleared the house; this time there were clear indications that we had disturbed someone when we had first moved into our cordon. A freshly fried plate of bacon sat on the floor, next to a revolting old mattress in a disgustingly smelly and ransacked room. Our targets had been living rough, all right. Unfortunately, I think the helicopter gave them the heads-up and they had slipped off early in the piece.

Finally, we went to the property on the other side of the target house. This time, we got a better result. The targets weren't there, but we located their stash of firearms poked through a hole in the back of a neighbouring shed. Recovering the .303 and .308 was a good result and although we had missed the targets themselves, it was a relief to now have their firearms in our possession.

Two weeks later, I had just spent a long and tiring week in court for a child abuse trial. It having started on Monday, by the Thursday afternoon I was keen for it to be over, as was the family involved. Also, during my week in court I was gutted to have missed two AOS training days. When the defence lawyer finally started summing up that Thursday afternoon, I left the courtroom and started walking back to the station, texting my husband as I went to let him know I was done for the day, and inviting him out for a run. 'I think the call-out is more important at the moment,' was his reply. I hadn't worn my pager in court as I wouldn't have been able to go anyway, but now I was free. *Yee-hah!* I ran the last 200 metres to the station and went straight to the squad room, but was somewhat confused to find that A was the only one there. He told me the pager had been set for a 4 p.m. call-out and it was still only 3.40 p.m. He had come down early because he was already floating around the station. The targets were to be our two Most Wanteds again.

I took the opportunity of an empty squad room to undress and get into my overalls without attracting any of the possible ribbing. By the time I had done this, the rest of the squad was starting to arrive. Our briefing, which was taken by my husband, was that we had new info about yet another address for one of the two targets. Both our targets were, apparently, now armed again.

It's never an issue for me when my husband is running the show, although I know he would hate it if I stuffed something up while he was in charge – barrelling out your own wife in a team debrief wouldn't be that much fun, so I always made extra sure I didn't do anything to bring attention to myself. There was a bit of stick from the others about my husband and me working together; mostly good-natured. He appeared to be well respected as a team leader, but I always felt that if he upset anyone too hugely they would have to wait for both of us to leave the squad room before they could have a decent moan.

We were split into our sections and assigned roles. I was to be on one side of the new target address along with T the dog handler, and I was also to carry a ladder. The stress of my week in court had already been replaced by adrenaline for the job we were facing.

With difficulty, I managed to fold myself, my ladder and my firearm into the small and very messy front seat of T's wagon. I was greeted by the overwhelming odour of dog, and apologies from T about how messy the vehicle was. I shoved dirty coffee cups and pieces of paperwork onto the floor to accommodate myself better. As we set off, we planned our entry. It was to be a screech to a halt, then both of us leaping out and taking up our points.

As we turned into the target's street, we got the signal to go. As soon as the vehicle had stopped, my door was open and I ran ahead. I nearly managed to overrun the address in my eagerness, but stopped in time and ran down into the back of a tidy section with fruit trees. As I rounded the corner, I looked to one side and saw the resident family start at my arrival; then, by the time I had reached the back corner of their property, they had all started to pour outside. At the same time, I could hear yelling from the other side of the property. It would appear that the team had already made contact with someone – hopefully our target.

I yelled at the family to go back inside and shut the door, and they complied straight away. My eyes widened at the sight of a large fence facing me along the side of the house – I could hear all the action but see nothing. I tried to get myself into a position to grab a possible runner. As I placed my ladder down, however,

I found I had a wee problem. It was a small extendable ladder and one of the pins that allowed it to collapse and open had worked its way into my glove. I tried to drop the ladder to the ground, but it stayed firmly attached to the wrist of my glove where it dangled like a large accessory.

I hazarded a glance in the direction of the family. All their faces were pressed up against their ranch slider, mouths agape, watching me. What a moment to look like a buffoon. Still nervously listening to the yelling on the other side of the property and wondering how I was going to chase someone with a ladder attached to my wrist, I ducked behind a tree so that the family couldn't see me, and frantically ripped at the pin.

It held firmly, as did my super-strong gloves, so I slung the ladder over my shoulder nonchalantly, like this was how it was meant to be. Some people choose to wear a wristwatch; I chose to wear a ladder. I would have to wait until the excitement on the other side of the fence had ended before trying to sort my kit, as to get the pin out would require two free hands and both eyes. I couldn't spare either at this moment. Yes, I could have taken the glove off. But I didn't. Don't ask me why not; I don't know. My mind works differently from the rest of the world.

Don't let him come my way just yet, I thought to myself. Although, if push came to shove, I'm sure I would have had no hesitation in sconing him with the ladder . . . or taking the glove off. After what seemed like forever, my earpiece announced that one of our Most Wanteds was now in custody. He had been seated out the back of the address, enjoying a cool beverage on a hot day, when Y had reached his pozzie over the side fence, within spitting distance of the target. On seeing the AOS, the target had immediately leapt to his feet and made to run to the back of the address. As he turned to do so, he saw S's large cranium poking up from over the back fence. Knowing that there was no way out, he put his hands in the air and gave up. His months of living on the run and eating cold bacon were over.

Gratefully, I took a moment to concentrate on removing the ladder pin from my glove, bearing in mind there was still the possibility of one more target in the house. Knowing that I might yet need the ladder, I resisted the temptation to add it to the burn pile the house occupants had in their backyard. For another 10 minutes I stood in the yard under the shade of an apple tree, waiting while a team cleared the house.

Before they announced it completely clear, however, I was indeed called forward with my trusty ladder. They told me they needed a ceiling cavity checked, and lucky old short-of-stature me got the job. The crawl space I was sent up into was swelteringly hot and had a height of about three-fifths of sod all. I belly-crawled my way over roof battens and around rafters, checking behind the water tank that was up there, using my Glock with its torch for both lighting and defence. But the ceiling was empty. By the time I was out of there and leaving the address, my face was as red as a beetroot from the heat and the exertion. This was, kindly, pointed out to me by a member of the inquiry team.

Back at the station, by which time I had cooled down considerably, I was chuffed at the team's result. We were now one offender down, with one still to locate. The next day, I returned to court as the jury went out to deliberate on the week's trial. The case involved the sexual abuse of children, and having watched four brave little souls stand up to a court's scrutiny earlier in the week, I was elated when, four hours after going out, the jury returned with their verdict. Guilty. My week was now complete.

23
ONE FOOT FORWARD

Just as some AOS jobs were straightforward, others gave clear indications early on that this wasn't going to be the case. Often, even after deployment, information would keep trickling in, creating a need for flexibility and flow in decision-making, as what you initially thought had happened might not be so at all.

A victim presenting himself at Accident and Emergency with a gunshot wound to his foot was the first, obvious, hint we had that someone had been shot. The indication that this wasn't a straightforward case wouldn't present itself until later.

As soon as the police were informed of this incident, the AOS were consulted and then we got the page. Finding out that a firearm had already been used on a person, as opposed to what we usually got – a firearm being 'presented' only – gave things an immediate air of reality. The exact circumstances it was used in, however, weren't yet clear. We had the victim's name and the fact that apparently he lived in the house the shot had been fired in. This house was in the same town where I had got stuck in the hedge, what seemed like years before.

Once the majority of the squad had turned up, we set off in various vehicles and all met up at the local police station. We were updated about any movements seen at the address (in this case there were none), then set off to the target's place. I was given one side of the house with G, with whom I always enjoy working. He is ex-army and has the ability to think very well tactically. He would always forge ahead of me, melting into shadows while I would be scratching my head trying to figure out how I could get past a thorny bush without getting stuck in it.

I was carrying the ladder, which experience told me I'd probably need – any fence over a metre was an obstacle for me. I was also wearing two new pieces of operational equipment that had just arrived. These were a new Kevlar helmet, which fitted perfectly, and a set of headphones that sat neatly under the helmet. This helmet, which was about 10 times better than the last one, didn't tilt forward all the time and, if I was lying prone, I could lift my head up without it knocking on the neck of my body armour and covering my eyes. The headphones were, however, the strangest piece of equipment I had ever used. They had noise amplifiers in them; when you put them on, you pushed a button that immediately turned your muffled world into a clearly heard world. A chip packet crinkling could be heard easily at a hundred metres, and birds chirping in the trees were deafening. The whole point of them, however, was that they muffled gunshots: a loud crack sounded like a dull thud. The only problem I had was it was difficult to gauge where a sound was coming from.

By the time G and I arrived at our drop-off point, there was still a bit of daylight left. We picked our way carefully along a back fence, which took us one property back and to the side of our target; then, hidden behind a large shed, we used the ladder to climb into the section next door. Once back on the ground, G tiptoed his way around the front of this neighbouring house, and I went around the back. Hugging the wall, I edged my way around the side until I had, while still partially hidden, a view of one side of the target's house.

From my position, I could see it clearly. It was a large old character home. There were maybe three big sash windows running down the side I was on, and a good-sized porch out the front. The whole place was reasonably well fenced, with a chest-height corrugated iron fence on my side, a large fence at the front, and a number of trees and shrubs all around the outside. Also on my side was a gravel driveway, which had a car parked in it facing out toward the street.

I saw a movement above me and, peeking up, caught a set of concerned eyes staring at me from the window of the house I was parked under. The man attached to the eyes was perhaps wondering what the hell I was doing in his backyard. I tiptoed backward and beckoned him over to his back door, then whispered to him that we were looking for his neighbours. Although terribly keen to help, he didn't have anything to add to our info. I told him to move across to the far side of his house and to stay there until we told him it was safe. Obediently he complied, quietly closing the door behind him, and I crept forward again to the corner of the house.

I heard the other squaddies calling in their positions and did the same, then heard one of our guys reporting movement toward the front of the house. I strained my eyes and ears to where they were, hearing lots of birds chirping with my magnified hearing but not much else. I then saw what they saw. Two guys had come out onto the front verandah and were walking toward the car. I could now hear their feet crunching on the gravel; then they came clearly into my view. Both of them were about medium height and size, and were walking side by side. Neither of them were carrying any firearms.

I knew that if I had to deal with them, I wasn't going to be able to get over that side fence at speed. I observed them for a moment, and watched as one of them went to the rear passenger door of the car. Someone from the front was calling these actions in as a commentary, and then Zero Alpha ordered that under no circumstances was the car to leave the address. If any move was made to the driver's side by either man, I would have to act quickly.

The male on the passenger side put a duvet or blanket into the back of the car, then both men disappeared back into the house. A few moments later, one of them re-emerged with a set of keys and headed to the driver's door, closely followed by the second one, who looked like he was going to be going along for the ride. Leaving me with bugger all time to think, they reached the car and began to get in, so I launched myself across the driveway toward them.

'Armed police! Armed police! Get your hands in the air!' I yelled at them while the passenger was folding himself into his seat. They both looked over the fence at me. Firearm raised, I continued yelling. The guy with the keys still had them in his hand, and was standing next to the unopened driver's door with a confused but interested look on his face. At least I had his full attention. The passenger was gazing over at me with an annoyed expression; perhaps I had interrupted them going to get a feed.

Slowly, as I continued yelling at them, they both put their hands in the air. One by one – starting with the driver – I told them to move to the front of the property, where someone else took over negotiations. The passenger extracted himself from his side of the car and, once clear of it, was directed over to where the driver now was. I turned my attention back to the house to make sure there were no more surprises about to walk out. There weren't.

Once the two were away from the house, it was cleared – there wasn't anyone else home. Then the inquiry team was called forward, and the mystery of who shot who and why began to unravel. The guy who had been shot in the foot was actually the aggressor of the whole mess. He had turned up with a firearm to cause a bit of stress in the house over the apparent shared love of a woman. He was on drugs, so wasn't very reasonable with the guy he was arguing with and had wound up in a fight. Somehow, in the struggle he got shot in the foot. Both of them had then gapped it, and the two we'd found were other flatmates who had decided the place was a bit hairy for them to stay at. Inspection of the house turned up blood and gunshot damage in the floor of the hallway, verifying the story. The guy with the shot foot didn't want to complain about anything and, at the time of writing, the guy who had pulled the trigger had not been found. And the woman at the centre of all this? Apparently oblivious to the whole drama.

24

THE FAME GAME

I'm not sure how true it is that everyone wants their 15 minutes of fame, but I have to admit that for me the idea is quite alluring. I reckon I might also like to extend it beyond 15 minutes, though; perhaps sneak 20 or 30 out of it.

The first question was, How I was going to do it? My husband's first question was, Why?

'To sell my book,' I answered. No one wants to buy a book if they have never heard of the author. If I drummed up enough pre-publicity, I might actually make some money out of it. Perhaps I might be able to embark on Hollywood as a new career, too? Without stopping to analyse things any further than this, I gave myself a week to do it in, and away I went. To get famous.

I had carried on painting in my spare time, and was making enough money out of selling a few of my masterpieces to buy the occasional cup of coffee, so thought I might begin there. Artist cum writer (the first book was actually still in the production phase then) cum mother cum copper. I thought I'd sell myself as a package. I put in a call to the local free-delivery newspaper. No sense getting ahead of myself too early by going bigger than a free local rag.

'Hi. I'm Liz Williams and I thought you might like to write a story about me.' I stopped there and was met with a stony silence, so, after an impolite pause (at her end), I continued my selling phase: 'It's just that I write and paint, and am a detective in the police . . . . and I'm a mother.' Silence. 'And that's about it.' Silence. 'Oh, and my book is getting published and my house is made of straw.'

Perhaps I had been too fragmented and she couldn't keep up. There was yet another period of silence at her end, by which time I was thinking she was just rude, then finally: 'That sounds interesting. I'll get someone to give you a ring then shall I?' I hung up, slightly deflated that I hadn't been snapped up immediately. I'd have thought the offered package was a sure winner.

Well, a week went by and I hadn't heard anything, so muttering rude words about the first woman I'd spoken to, I rang the opposition free newspaper. This was going to be a long project, but the first paper's loss was going to be the second paper's gain. I did my lines, was transferred to someone else, who again listened in silence, then I was told 'That sounds interesting', and was given more assurances that I would be phoned. *Yeah right*, I thought to myself. *I wonder if other 'getting famous' people have to work this hard.*

Another week crept past. At this rate, there was no way I was going to be famous by Friday.

Finally, I got a phone call and the reporter and I arranged a meeting at a local café. 'I'm going to be interviewed by the newspaper,' I told the café owner as I sat waiting at a table in the corner. She was much more enthusiastic than the newspaper reporters I'd spoken to, although I was too embarrassed to admit to her that I had actually masterminded the whole thing. I might just as well have admitted I was going on a reality TV show.

As I sat there waiting, I got another call. It was the newspaper lady saying that she couldn't make it. *Super*. I drained my coffee and disappeared into the oblivion of being me.

Another week went by, and another meeting was set up. This time, I had to cancel – something crazy like police work got in the way. Finally, we arranged what was to be our third and final appointment. It was the same café, and once again I told the owner that today was the day I would become famous.

I had taken along my visual diary (where I do all my doodling for painting ideas), and was scribbling happily away. I was sitting in a discreet corner, so as not to look too loser-like sitting by myself. I then started clock-watching, and waiting. I had no idea what this reporter looked like and, presumably, as I wasn't yet famous, she wouldn't know what I looked like either. Maybe she was already there. I scanned the crowd, but no one looked like they were lost or looking for someone to make famous.

I immersed myself in doodling and checked my watch after a while. Twenty minutes late. The amount of time I'd predicted I was going to be famous for had just been wasted waiting. I had been stood up. How rude. I decided I would remember them when I was rich and famous, and planned my next attack on fame.

Maybe I was aiming too low? Perhaps the local paper that you had to pay for was more likely to snap me up. I put in my phone call, and was somewhat mollified when they actually appeared enthusiastic. Yet another interview was set up, at home, and this time, to my surprise, the reporter actually showed up. The only trouble was, I had set up my little easel, applied a little lippy and preened myself ever so slightly, only to find he hadn't brought a photographer with him (if my witty dialogue didn't catch them, I'd been aiming for looks by getting photographed). The photos were apparently happening on another day.

Carefully placing his Dictaphone on the table between us, the reporter fired a few questions at me. Although I realised that talking about me was the whole point of the exercise, I felt somewhat of a prat as I jabbered on. I had sounded so much more interesting when I'd talked about me in my own head.

The world is actually very little when it's broken down, and when the reporter and I started talking I learnt that his new son-in-law was an old Air Force mate of mine. That filled in 10 minutes. Also, this reporter had covered the Lundy trial, which I had worked on as well – that covered another 10 minutes. Then we wrapped it up. My 20 minutes was up.

I ended our afternoon by walking him out to his car – helping him to step over the Helens as we went. The Helens are my chickens. They all look the same, so I call them all Helen – after my sister-in-law, not the former Prime Minister. He successfully avoided the hens but, as we finished up our farewells, he absently leant against the fence that kept my wild, crazy miniature pony from escaping, and it bit him.

I cringed in anticipation of the tirade of abuse the reporter was about to hurl at the pony, but he very politely smiled and rubbed at his injured digit with just a 'I forgot little horses did that.' I grimaced in reply. He was going to slate me in his article now. *Stupid little horse.*

Two days after that, I smiled and posed while I was snapped by the paper's photographer, paintbrush dripping with paint, dabbing at my latest canvas creation. I tried to give my face a look of . . . well, I'm not sure what I was aiming for. As I posed and painted, the small world kept right on shrinking as the photographer told me how I reminded him of my mum – he used to work with her at another newspaper, apparently. Luckily, he liked her.

So, they printed the story about me in the paper. I was now a half-page of nearly being famous. But I felt like I needed something else. Fifteen minutes wasn't nearly enough.

My second crack at the fame game came about at the new Palmerston North police station Open Day some months later. The rush for my presence at every possible speaking engagement following my foray into the medium of print had by then died down (yes, I jest), and I was spending this Saturday at work in the role of a CIB information kiosk officer, telling visitors all about what the duties of a police officer in the CIB involved. We had cordoned off the CIB office area and I sat primly behind a desk just inside the no-go zone, getting stared at by a stream of people who were filing through. I felt like a national treasure.

During one quiet moment, I was speaking with a woman who worked at Police National Headquarters in Wellington. She had something to do with the *Police Ten 7* TV series, and for that day was incarcerated in a small room next door to where I was caged, on a police recruiting stand. As we chatted generally, she started asking me if I might be interested in a new recruiting video they were putting together. She said they were looking for young-looking female police officers, and thought I could be filmed giving a briefing to other staff about some exciting warrant, or the like. Without wishing to look too excited, I told her, 'Yes! That sounds very exciting!' Okay, so I'm pretty transparent. At the end of the day, she took my e-mail address and disappeared; *Probably never to be heard of again*, I thought to myself.

About two months later, however, she phoned and said the *Police Ten 7* crew were coming up to Palmerston North to film a night-shift, and would I be available for a screen test? *A screen test? Whoa! Here I come!*

I cleared my diary for the evening, and spent a bit of time filling in the crow's feet around my eyes with some putty. I was confident that I could at least pass for 25 (I was 34 then). Arriving at the station on time, I walked into the room, but immediately started sweating profusely upon seeing the big camera and tripod facing in my direction.

Previously unbeknownst to me, I discovered that when confronted with such a frightening situation, I am one of those people who talk even more than normal – which for me is lots anyway. Nervously I pressed my fingers to my temples (in an effort to push the putty back into place, as opposed to relieving tension), and then I started to talk, and talk, and talk. I couldn't shut myself up. I introduced myself to everyone in the room at least twice; then, when I was introduced to some man from Australia (the head of the Queensland Police, I believe), I praised the work of the New Zealand Police like I was the one responsible for how great we all were, as if I was our leader or something. *Good lord.*

Finally, they decided to do the screen test. I was to be interviewed about what seemed now to be my favourite topic. Me. I think I did all right up to the point where I decided to go off on a tangent. Knowing that the Australian police boss was at the back of the room (he was there that night for something entirely different from my moment of glory), I deviated to talking about the fact that I was actually Australian by birth. And that I was really proud to be Australian by birth. And that I was born in Newcastle, which is in Queensland.

Now, anyone who knows even the smallest thing about geography, would know that Newcastle is in New South Wales, not Queensland. And I'm sure the majority of the population also knows where they were born. That night, I didn't. (Perhaps the worst aspect of this faux pas was that I only realised what I'd said as I was reliving the experience while driving home.)

After the initial off-camera interview, I was then told to do a straight-to-camera talk. I had to stare down the barrel, and talk. 'About what?' I asked. 'Anything,' the man said. I thought I'd already said everything I had to say during my off-camera interview thingy, and was now going to have to find something else. In a stroke of stupidity, I announced that I was going to do a speech to the local Rotary club in a couple of nights' time (I actually was), so perhaps I could use that? 'Great,' said the man. 'Do that.'

The problem about the Rotary speech, though, was that I didn't actually have one. I'd had a late invite (the more interesting speaker they'd lined up had pulled out), and thought I could get through by winging it. So, for my screen test, without any time to drum up something imaginative, I started prattling. And I was dreadful. If I said it once, I think I said 10 times how great Palmy was – despite what John Cleese and Rhys Darby both thought, and that I was a cop, and that I liked policing and painting, although not necessarily in that order . . . blah, blah, blah. Cut.

I scurried off and relived this ordeal over and over in my head for the next day or two. I thought about resigning from the police due to the embarrassment I'd caused them. About four months went by, and I hadn't heard a thing about whether they wanted to use me or not. The latter was most likely the case, but I had to know. I sent off an e-mail to the woman who had put me in this pickle in the first place.

Her chirpy reply came back. Yes, I did look 34 and not 25. No, they hadn't noticed the Australian thing (they were, perhaps, focusing on how much I talked and what crap I came out with). And no, they weren't going to use me.

So 15 minutes it is.

25

THE NAPIER SIEGE 2009

7 May 2009. Three days shy of Mother's Day. Five days short of my thirty-eighth birthday. Winter was on its way, and spending time indoors in warm houses and offices was preferable to standing out in the cold. I had managed to get to work on time that day – a rarity when the six-year-old in the house procrastinates in everything, from putting his shoes on, to eating his breakfast, to making his bed, to opening his curtains. The solution was easy. I left it all to my husband and went in to work early.

I had one small goal I had to achieve in the next eight hours: to lock up a chronic inner-city menace. The menace in question usually spent his days in town hovering around the money machine, hitting up users for money as soon as they had made their withdrawal. As I don't know of any money machines that dispense coins, he was making a killing. Most days he would net about $40. Nice work if you can get it.

The crux of the complaint against him, however, was that in order not to lose his prime position on Bankers' Corner when he needed to pee, instead of walking across the road to the public toilets he would disappear up an alleyway next to 'his bank' and urinate there. Many local businesses used this alleyway when people had their work breaks, and as this guy would often urinate in front of them as they were biting into their ham and cheese sandwiches, he was committing offences.

After doing a couple of laps around the city centre looking for him without success, I then went to his house. It appeared that he had decided to have a day in and was at home watching DVDs. With his permission, I carted him back to the police station to have a chat about his toileting practices; then I heard the breaking news. Three, perhaps four, police officers had been shot in Napier by an armed gunman. My heart dropped.

The early news was sketchy. It was believed that one officer was dead, and that perhaps the other two were seriously injured, as well as one civilian possibly injured. The offender was holed up in his house, which was surrounded by the Napier AOS, and he was still firing indiscriminately at police.

Frustratingly, when all I wanted to do was hear more about the events unfolding, I still had to interview my urinater. As I did so, my attention wandered throughout. Despite my best efforts, and although he had admitted to the offences he was accused of, when I later reviewed it the interview was pretty rubbish. When it was over, I took him to the cells area and handed him over for the arrest process, then headed off to the senior sergeant's office for any updates.

My husband was there, along with P, the other senior who ran the AOS squad. My first question was 'Can I go?', as I knew it was highly likely we would be sending an AOS contingent over. 'No,' P told me. 'I've already selected the team and you're not in.' I was gutted.

Why did I want to go? Lots of reasons. Mainly, the fact that cops had been shot, and were still getting shot at. Every other cop wanted to be part of resolving what had happened to our fellow members of the police. The officer who was believed to have received fatal wounds was still at the scene, as the area was too dangerous to bring him out. I didn't know him but he was still a colleague, and I, like many others, just wanted to get in and bring him out.

As P was going to be running the contingent that went to Hawke's Bay, my husband would be left with an AOS skeleton crew in Palmerston North. There was still a pending job he was responsible for, so he would have to keep an eye on that. I pleaded my case to go again, to P's seemingly deaf ears, then left their office to tidy up my urinater's file for court.

Twenty minutes later I got a phone call from P. Along with eight other personnel from Palmerston North squad and three from Wanganui, I would be among the team that would be leaving at 4 p.m. from a park in town in two Iroquois helicopters. My immediate thought was how privileged I was to be part of this. Terror wasn't to kick in until later.

I sorted out trivial things at work, with the knowledge that I might not be back for a few days, then let our friends the Newtons know about the imminent chopper trip. I asked them if they could bring my wee one down to see me off. I knew it wouldn't be the usual, 'See you soon, buddy – Mummy's got to go to the office to shuffle some paperwork now; don't forget to brush your teeth.'

We were only allowed to take a small amount of clothing, so I packed one spare set of black overalls, a couple of pairs of underpants and a toothbrush. I was wearing full AOS kit with extra supplies of smoke and stun grenades, spare radio and torch batteries. We all headed down to the park for our ride. My husband was the driver of the AOS truck that transported us down there, and from the look on his face I knew he was gutted not to be going with us.

At the park, there were a few intermediate-aged kids having sports practice on one side of the field, who showed some interest in our arrival. Showing a bit more interest were the slightly worried-looking parents who were with them. Armed police on a kids' sports field isn't a good look.

'Hello, Mum.' I looked over at the sound of the little voice. My wee guy was standing there with a bemused look on his face. I don't think he'd ever seen me in full kit before and must have been a bit intimidated. I peeled off from the team that was heading out onto the field, and went over to him. Going along with the cover story suggested by my friends, I told him I was off to do some AOS training but I'd see him really soon. I went to give him a hurried kiss goodbye, and in doing so smacked him in the forehead with the rim of my Kevlar helmet. *Please don't let him cry, please don't cry*, I thought to myself.

While I wanted to go on this job, I also felt guilty for going and leaving my husband and son behind. I jollied my boy along to keep him happy, then with a smile and a wave ran off to join the team now lined up waiting for the helis to touch down. I didn't dare look back.

We crowded around P for a last briefing; then, on the stroke of 4 p.m., heard the impending arrival of our rides. In two sections of six, we dropped to one knee in a line facing where the choppers would come down. Due to the size of our group and the amount of kit we would carry, we needed two. We had one AOS dog handler with us – M, who was in the other group with his police dog.

The last time I had been in a confined space with a police dog had been at an AOS helicopter training day a few weeks previously. We had practised climbing in and then bringing the dog in while the chopper was static. I had been put in the front next to the pilot, facing the rear, and the dog was shoved in with his arse facing me. To my horror, I saw them try to pull the door closed with the dog's tail draped across the door's slide rail. I knew what its response would be – a pain-induced overreaction consisting of frenzied biting of anything in reach.

I quickly picked his tail up, holding it gingerly between two gloved fingers; then, in a stroke of spectacularly bad timing, the handler, T, moved his foot to get more comfortable and stomped on the remaining bit of tail that was more closely connected to the dog's body. The animal's head spun around and his angry canine eyes met mine as he took in the view of me holding the end of his stomped-on tail. I felt like a kid who had been caught with their hand in the lolly jar. With a guilty return look at the dog, I quickly dropped his people-greeter, the door was closed safely and the crisis was averted.

The dog on today's trip was of pretty much the same ilk as T's dog, so I was happy he was in chopper B. As the two Iroquois landed side by side in front of us, we received the thumbs-up from the crewie and everyone filed forward. F was in front of me, and the last one in the stack – P – was behind me. As nimbly as I could in my bulky kit, I clambered up. While P climbed onto the side-facing seat nearest the back, F – who was a reasonably fat bastard – hogged nearly the entire rest of the tiny seat I was to be on, leaving me perched on the outer edge with just millimetres between me and the heli's lip. I tried vainly to shuffle myself closer into F's side, managed to secure the small safety belt into place, and moments later the helicopter started lifting off the ground in a lazy hover. Next to us the second Iroquois was doing the same.

By now we had the full attention of the kids playing sports. They had stopped kicking balls around and were lined up as if for inspection, watching the spectacle unfolding in front of them. One very brave young lad defiantly turned around, whipped his shorts to his knees and slapped his bum cheeks provocatively at the hovering helis. I had to admire the audacity of the little rat, but I also hoped the downdraft of the rotors would dislodge a small pebble to give his bare bum a reminder of why bare skin and rotors shouldn't be within 30 metres of each other. And that he should respect his elders – especially when they were armed.

The door was still open as the heli got higher and I felt in danger of falling outside, so I leaned my arm across to grasp F's thigh holster as a means of holding on. As we cleared the city and started flying toward Napier, I kept grabbing then releasing F's holster (and no – that's not a euphemism for anything) as we hit pockets of turbulence. The second Iroquois was dipping and diving in front of us in much the same manner. The ride was brief – 40 minutes. As we headed into Napier, I could see in front of us Hospital Hill – where the gunman was still holed up.

Immediately after landing, we regrouped next to the vehicles that would ferry us to the army base we would work out of. It was at the foot of Hospital Hill. After loading up, we drove through a number of police roadblocks around the base of the hill. It was immediately clear that the gunman was controlling a large area.

Within metres of the army base, we came across a huge media contingent. As the initial hours progressed into days their numbers would swell even further, and every time we drove through as we were ferried back and forth to and from the hot zone, camera flashes went off and video cameras were pointed toward our vehicles. As I had only heard about what had happened from police sources, I hadn't seen any media reporting at all, and hadn't realised the enormity of what we were going into. This started to bring it all home.

As soon as we rolled into the yard that first time, we climbed out of the van, and within five minutes of standing there I heard the first sign of things to come. Three high-powered-rifle shots could be clearly heard. Apparently the guy was still shooting at the staff surrounding his house. It was a very sobering sound.

We placed our kit down and were directed toward a food stand. The Salvation Army had set up a caravan and a couple of tents out the front of the army base, and in the time we were there supplied us with a continual source of hot, plentiful food. What an amazing bunch of people. I knew they were all giving their time for nothing, and the sight of some of the volunteers who were still in school uniform impressed the hell out of me. The contribution of these schoolkids made the boy who'd done the brown-eye look even more like a disrespectful moron.

We chugged down some food, savouring its warmth as much as we could. We were eager to learn more about what had been happening and what would be required of us, but we also knew that wherever we ended up we weren't likely to have a ready supply of hot nosh.

By now it was about 5.30 p.m., so we had a briefing to update us on the state of play. It wasn't encouraging information. Police negotiators hadn't been able to contact the gunman yet, and the loud hailer used by surrounding AOS members had been shot at. There was info to suggest the shooter had an arsenal and was prepared for a showdown. The calibre of his firearms was varied, and by the sound of the one we had heard on our arrival at least one was high-powered. The murdered police officer was still outside the address and it was still too dangerous to retrieve him. AOS teams were in surrounding cordons, but anyone who lifted their head was getting shot at.

Our team's first role was to go in under cover of darkness and replace the first response squad, from the Napier AOS. They had been in position since 9.30 that morning – without food, getting shot at, and with the knowledge that one of their people was lying below them, most probably dead.

As night fell, we assembled and checked each other's kit. God, I was nervous. Policing is a crazy job. When the shit hits the fan, the normal reaction is to turn and run. Today I had to fight that urge (and believe me it was a big urge, regardless of the volunteering aspect) and march forward against the flow. I grabbed the camo face paint I usually carried but had never used before and plastered my face with it, not wishing for any part of my whiter-than-white Caucasian skin to shine out in the darkness. I also taped over a couple of the press studs on my kit where the black had worn off, as in the darkness they would act as shiny magnets for light; under no circumstances did I want to be seen. I wore multiple layers of clothing and wet-weather gear, as it was a very cold night. Lying still on cold ground for what could be many hours was going to be taxing.

Once sorted, our team climbed into our varying transports and moved forward through the media, public and roadblocks. The road we took wound up and around the back of the target's address in a confusing, meandering route. I quickly became disorientated as the road turned back on itself and then forked off in yet another direction. If you'd given me a map and told me to point north I would have been stuck. All too soon, however, we were at our SFP – safe forward point.

Leaving the warm sanctuary of the car, we paired off. I was with G, the sniper, and our position was to be in the property behind the target address. We were given this property's street number and walked off into the darkness, eyes constantly scanning to our right where the offender's address was, somewhere below us, ready to drop if we heard any shots. On reaching the designated driveway, we edged our way quietly down it, then around the side of a house. This route took us out to the back of the target's house, elevated high above it because of the lay of the land.

Quietly and slowly, we crept forward to a hedge that ran along the fence on the offender's house boundary. Reaching it, I dropped to my knees and tried to find the best position for view along with, most importantly, cover from fire. I carefully pushed grass aside, snapping a few twigs to give a limited, partial view to the rear and right side of his house, the best I could manage in the circumstances. The offender's section was terraced going downhill from where we were, and each terrace sloped and appeared to drop about a storey down to the next. Our location at the rear was probably about four storeys higher than the main house. Slightly to our left, about 10 metres away, was a smaller hut, also on the offender's property. Other AOS members were set up near this; although indications were that he was holed up in the main house, this small hut at the rear couldn't yet be ruled out of play.

Once I had established the optimum sniper spot, I motioned for G to move in. He lowered himself to the ground then shuffled forward to the fence line, poking the muzzle of his rifle through the hole I had made, settling in a prone position. I hunched down beside him with the NVGs and we began the wait. Behind and around me, I could hear the shuffling of other squaddies also moving into their positions. The last shots fired had been on our arrival at the base; by now that was over two hours ago. Who knew when the next would be?

We settled in for a long night, G and I alternating positions occasionally. At one point I moved about 6 metres further along to try to get a better view, but after sitting there for about half an hour and constantly reassessing where I was in terms of vantage and cover, I manoeuvred back to G again. The position he was in was still the best.

I was nervous, and wary about where the offender might appear from if he did choose to come our way. Did he have a little path through the vegetation in his backyard that we couldn't see from our vantage point? Was he intending to stay and fight or would he try to escape? Did he have a secret tunnel from his house to the hut in front of us that we didn't know about? Despite my overanalysing of the situation, however, I was reasonably confident that if he did move toward us he would be making a hell of a racket when he navigated the dense vegetation on the other side of the hedge, and he would be seen from the other positions held by the AOS teams.

As G and I lay there, we could hear the eerie sound of the murdered officer's pager, which kept beeping a 10-minute reminder as he lay there outside the address. When the call was made after the shooting, all Napier AOS pagers had been set off; the victim was an AOS member and had been wearing his at the time. The beeping noise was a constant reminder of why we were there, and created in me a feeling of intense sadness for the murdered man followed by intense anger at the offender's actions, which had led to this man's senseless death and the serious injuries of his workmates and an innocent member of the public.

As I waited, I was deliberately only having the occasional sip of water, as the issue of the toilet was one hassle I didn't need. Although I was wearing my specially adapted overalls, the situation I was currently in didn't lend itself to peeling off for a pee in the bush. By now the cold had also started to set in, and I began to shake uncontrollably. Occasionally, I rolled onto my back and tucked my gloved hands under my arms, my M4 resting by my side, but the cold continued to seep through my clothing unabated.

Lying on my side wasn't much better, and after a time the discomfort began to get a bit demoralising. G and I fuelled ourselves with the multiple snacks I was carrying, scoffing a bag of gummi-snakes and packets of crackers with cheese dip. My spirits lifted with the sugar, but all too soon this was replaced with more shivering. I tried to cosy up next to G, but he was having none of it. Probably my sapping of what little body heat he had wasn't the best – if anyone needed a steady focus and to avoid shaking at the required moment, it was him. Also, I don't think it was the done thing for AOS members to cuddle when on a cordon. I would have to sort myself out.

Meanwhile, below us other squaddies were calling in occasional activity from the offender. He wasn't presenting himself as a target – instead, he was flicking outside lights on and off in a taunting fashion. At about midnight, my earpiece reported that the negotiators had finally made contact with the target. His moods were ranging through many differing emotions. After some time this initial contact was severed, so we continued to wait for his next move, having no idea what it would be.

I stood occasionally, concealed from view behind the hedge, with the NVGs held against my eyes to get a better view of the rear of the yard, but on every occasion saw no movement. As the late night turned into early morning, I lay on my back next to G, closing my eyes to try to rest. Continually staying in a high state of anticipation is draining. As long as I was being cocooned by the biting cold I knew I wasn't going to fall asleep, but the act of closing my eyes helped me relax, even if it was only for a few moments. Taking turn about with this, G did the same thing. There had been no signs of lights or movement for quite a while. Then, suddenly, that changed.

Without warning, the silence was shattered by the staccato cracks of a .22-calibre firearm. My eyes shot open, as wide as saucers, and I didn't dare move. The first volley of shots hadn't hit me, so I figured not moving meant not drawing attention to myself – clearly the safest option. Sensing no movement from me, G dug me in the ribs with his elbow and told me to wake up. I didn't answer because I was trying to figure out which direction the continuing shots were aimed in. As I lay on my back, as still as I could be, it seemed to me to be just off to my right, as I thought I heard one round connect with something nearby. I just hoped it wasn't one of us. The radio chatter sparked up between our positions, with the shots being reported to Zero Alpha.

Thinking I was sleeping through it all, I got another dig in the ribs from G. To stop his digs from getting harder I slowly rolled over toward him, trying to keep my movements slow so as not to attract any attention. We had a quick whispered conversation. Neither of us could figure out where the shots had gone to or come from. I kept my head down throughout. The last thing I wanted was a round through the top of my helmet.

After a short spell, the shooting stopped. My breathing slowed again, and I began to feel less tense. I tried once more to get a better view beside G, but still seeing nothing, settled down again to wait. At least with the offender firing shots, we could confirm he was still in the house. I also tried to rationalise why he had used the .22 when he had a larger calibre with him. Was he trying to let us know he was there but not wanting to cause much damage to us, by going with smaller rounds? Over the next spell of time – it was difficult to tell how long – we got another few bursts from the same firearm, fired seemingly randomly although one shot took out a street light near the front of the address. Where he could, he was clearly deliberately focusing.

More lights went on and off at the house with no one seen, followed by a long, quiet spell. Then I heard the worst sound imaginable – the crack of a high-powered rifle. He must have had it on semi-auto, as there were about eight shots in rapid succession fired to the left of our location. It was awful – the sound, the fact that it was obvious he wanted to hit one of us, and the intensity of the noise in the still night. The .22 had seemed bad enough, but this was another league altogether. My shivering from the cold became shivering from fright as I gripped the stock of my M4, laid myself as flat as I could against the cold earth, and hoped like hell he wasn't taking aim in our direction.

After a bit the shooting stopped again. G suggested I try to get a better look by getting higher. 'Fuck off,' I retorted, through gritted teeth. Any getting up above cover was, in my eyes, potentially fatal. I had already tried to obtain a better view of the offender's backyard in the early part of our shift, without success. We were too far above him, the bank partially obscured the rear of his house, and there was too much vegetation leading back to our position that I couldn't see through. Senselessly sticking my head up now was not going to make the crap view any less crap. We were only going to be effective if he clearly presented himself or ventured up our way.

I'll pause here to introduce you properly to G, my partner on this night. While he was a laugh-a-minute kind of guy in normal circumstances, when we were deployed operationally he was serious, professional and an excellent operator. A laid-back Maori dude, he had been on the squad for a few years longer than me. His sense of humour and casual attitude were unrivalled and, in the tenseness of that night, his presence was like a soothing balm. If he wasn't ruffled, then I wasn't. If he started to panic, then the situation would have to be really bad. As the night wore on, he happily scuffled around in the food pouch I carried, ferreting for something to eat, calm as a calm thing. His sneezing some time after the large-calibre-arm fire nearly made me shit myself, as our cocoon of safe silence was betrayed by his sinuses. I cringed, expecting a volley of shots, but got nothing. Again, I thought to myself, 'Well, if G's not worried, then neither am I.'

After the rifle shots, there was much more silence. Much, much more silence. It was suspense-filled, though. I didn't know when the next action would be, so was unable to relax. It was a relief to hear that the negotiators were trying to call the offender again – something different that was happening to break the night down into more manageable emotional chunks.

When the radio in my ear was transmitting, at times I could hear the negotiator in the background, talking to the target. I recognised the negotiator's voice – it was Z. I was confident that if negotiation had the chance to end all this, then they had the right man doing the job. Z would do everything to look after us and protect us in our vulnerable positions. But the gunman didn't want to talk much, and after a while he left the phone off the hook, or something, and could no longer be reached. So we waited.

Toward 4 a.m., the news reached us that the next shift were due in at 5.30 a.m. After the cold and the night's drama, it was welcome news. G and I continued as we were, lying there, watching and waiting. Close to 5.30, before the sun began to rise, we heard the radio crackling with dialogue. The replacements had arrived. I left my spot and walked back to them, led them to our location and we briefed them on their arcs of fire, best vantage points, and exactly where the area of operation was below us. After many clarifying questions, G and I got up and made our way out.

Walking the short distance back to our ride got the blood circulating and I began to feel better. We all climbed into the car and turned the heater on to get some more warmth back into our bones. Everyone was chilled through, but despite the tiredness and cold we all talked over what had happened at our individual vantage points. Having been used to the advantage of surprise, with us having the upper hand at most AOS jobs I had been deployed on, getting shot at was a surreal experience.

One of the guys captured perfectly how I'd felt. He said an SAS friend of his once remarked that people who say that when you're fired upon your training just takes over and you react, are talking a load of crap. In fact, he went on to say, all you want to do is bury your head down out of the firing line and get out alive. The only time it would be different was if you were fighting for your life; if it was either them or you, and to not fight back meant death. That SAS guy sounded like a wise man.

By now the sun was up, and a new day had begun. After de-kitting, our next priority was to get hot food inside us, so we trooped out to the front of the base HQ to visit the wonderful Sally Army legends with all the refreshments. Following that, after filling out required paperwork, we arranged vehicles and set off to a motel that had a number of rooms set aside for us. En route, I tried to get some of my face paint off with a wet paper towel. After this operation, amid lots of jocularity from my fellow squaddies, it was pointed out that I'd left a set of huge, blackened eyebrows behind – worthy of Groucho Marx.

At the motel I was rooming with a female police negotiator from Palmy, so once we had our assigned room key we set off to get some kip. Like the Sallys parked out in front of HQ, the motelier was incredibly good to us. They had been carrying out building renovations at their place, but on our arrival and knowing we were to be sleeping through the day, they kindly halted the use of all noisy power tools for as long as we required it. Rudely, I repaid their kindness by using their pristine white facecloths to try to dislodge the thick stripes of camo paint from my eyebrows.

I struggled to get out of the motel's shower, its warmth chasing away the cold discomfort I had been feeling for the previous 14 hours. If the chairs in the unit had been plastic, I would have dragged one in and sat on it under the piping-hot water; as it was, it took half an hour of wonderful hot shower before I felt I was both physically and mentally able to get out.

Sleep was difficult. I replayed the night over and over in my dreams. Whenever I woke up – which was often – I would turn on my police radio to see if anything new was happening. Intermittently between naps, I fired off texts to friends and family to let them know I was all right, and eagerly awaited news of the gunman giving up or of the retrieval of the murdered police officer. There were now reports that a police dog called Fi was still in her handler's van parked out the front of the offender's address. It was thought she might be dead; apparently she was normally very vocal, but since the siege began hadn't made a sound from the back of the van. I willed her to be okay, too.

I gave the sleep thing up after about three hours. When I emerged from my room I found the rest of the squad doing much the same thing, wandering around the motel and trying to get updates. We were told we would have to be kitted up and ready to go again at 4.30 p.m., so after cleaning my kit from the night's crawling around in the bushes and polishing off a breakfast consisting of more of the muesli bars I had snacked on during the night, I and the others headed off to the base again.

Things had revved up a bit. There seemed to be more people around than before, and many familiar faces that I had come across in the course of my police career. We were all here for the same reason: we couldn't bear the thought of not being there. After a further detailed briefing with the day's updates, we were allocated roles again. This time G and I would be at the front of the house, down near the bottom of the street. This position afforded a better view and was more suitable for the sniper role. It had also worn a few of the rounds from the previous evening's firing. I hoped we weren't going to be coming up against the same again this night.

As night fell we watched the army's LAV (light armoured vehicle) roll out of the yard with a contingent on board. They were going to get the fallen officer. We stood there quietly, listening to the radio chatter about their progress. Some time later the gates opened and they rolled back in again, our colleague on board. No one from the squad said a word. We just stood there in a darkened corner of the yard, watching the LAV back up into a hangar. Before he was brought out many of us wandered off, feeling that it was disrespectful to be just standing there watching. By the time we returned, the CIB had shown up and had begun their role. Twenty minutes later we saddled up and headed out again. If we were looking for time to reflect on what had just happened, it wasn't going to be then.

G and I were dropped within metres of our position. Utilising banks and bushes for cover, we moved in and, as we had the night before, set ourselves up with the best possible view. This time we had a low brick wall to shelter behind as well as a lot of shrubbery, but to get a view of the front we had to make an unavoidable break from cover. In the briefing earlier that evening, we had been told that the gunman was possibly dead after taking his own life that afternoon, but there was no way to confirm this. Until it *was* confirmed, we had to treat the threat as just as high as the night before.

This time I sat at our vantage point with the NVGs while G either lay prone with his rifle, slightly behind me and to the side, or sat behind cover and rested. I was even more uncomfortable than on the previous night. We were on a slight rise trying to look up the street, and it wasn't long before the cold set in again despite the fact that I was wearing even more clothing. When I took cover and G took over observation, my eyes started seeing things. I watched the branches of a nearby tree turn into a lion being fed by a fat woman wearing something that looked like an air mattress around her waist. I saw a small swarm of black-and-white-striped spiders flying toward me (I'm not sure how they flew, as they had no wings), but before they got to me, they peeled off. (Perhaps to bother someone else at another cordon point.)

I also saw a group of shadows continually moving in a conservatory or similar in a house high up behind us, but learnt later that I hadn't been seeing things there. This was real – apparently a camera was filming the entire thing from the high point. I was rather gobsmacked that people could be so foolish as to put themselves into a position that could be seen by this offender.

By now it was raining. During my times off guard, I stood up and walked back up a track that wound behind the cemetery opposite the offender's house, windmilling my freezing hands and arms above my head to try to warm them up. The track was steep, and walking up it allowed the blood to circulate again. On these trips, I encountered the Wanganui dog handler who had hurried up and was waiting behind cover. Stopping to furnish him with food (I've said it before and I'll say it again – stick with the girls on stake-outs: they are always prepared), we chatted about the night.

We were far enough away that we could talk without being heard at the offender's address, and I felt safe with the cover of a large hillside between him and us. I wished I could have had a police dog on nights like this. I would have it tucked in next to me and would be making full use of its warmth. After every visit to the handler's spot I would begrudgingly return to my cold, wet post to observe some more. If I'd been certain it didn't bite people, I would have taken his dog along for both G and me.

Following the successful recovery of the murdered officer's body, a decision was made to try for the police dog, Fi, who was still in the van. Although there was a strong possibility she was dead, her rescue still had to be tried. This was timed to coincide with the arrival of an army robot, which we were all calling Wall-E. He was a tremendous little thing. Watching his performance from afar, I'm sure I could be forgiven for thinking he was real, with his own personality. Listening to him (or 'it', I guess) doing his thing, it felt like progress was being made. Instead of being held to ransom on the gunman's say-so, it felt like we were able to be proactive without risking more officers' lives. It was great.

Then came a wonderful, wonderful sound. As I listened to Wall-E smashing something at the offender's property I caught a whining noise. There were a few dogs in properties around the target, but I had only ever heard them barking. This sound was quite different, and it sounded like it was coming from the dog wagon. Fi must have heard the sounds Wall-E was making and given out a small reminder that she was still there. She wasn't overtly giving her position away; more reminding anyone who cared that she'd quite like some time-out soon as she needed to pee, eat and have a run around – in no particular order.

As Wall-E did his thing around the house, we waited for the news that the gunman's dead body had been found, which would progress things for us in terms of safety. So far no joy, however. Wall-E went back to his operator for refreshments while a team moved forward to see what they could do for Fi. Through the NVGs I watched them pop open the back of the dog van, then kept watching with delight as Fi leapt out. From my vantage point, her reaction to their presence seemed to be akin to 'Who the hell are you lot? Where's my boss?' She ran around them warily, looking up at the looming shapes of fully kitted-up members, then shot up the road a bit. Frantic whispers of 'Fi! Fi, come here Fi!' were issuing from everyone in her vicinity.

In confusion, she turned around and ran part-way up the neighbours' drive. I listened in frustration to the whistles and calls to her, and at last she headed down toward them – only to then turn around and bugger off back up the road again! It was maddening to watch. Finally one of the team grabbed her and got her on a lead, and they moved back to our cordon point. The dog sergeant took Fi off them and I could hear the absolute delight in his voice as he chatted away to her, leading her back to his van with her bouncing at his side. It was a real feel-good moment for me, and gave a ray of light in what was a terrible two days.

Once the excitement had died down and Fi had been whisked off, I watched Wall-E trundling back down the road again. I was looking forward to his next manoeuvre; however, almost to my annoyance, our relief showed up at this point.

As they moved forward to our position, we briefed them about what had been happening in our cordon point, and I then waved my hand in the direction of a left-over and now cold mince dish that I had brought with me from the food angels about 12 hours before. It had become less appealing during the night as it got cold and congealed. I told the dog handler who was replacing me that they were welcome to help themselves. 'Too late,' he told me sheepishly. I turned to see the last of it being gobbled down by his dog.

G and I moved back out of our position, crashing through the undergrowth to again utilise cover on our retreat. Through my earpiece I could hear the changing of the guard of a number of positions, and was glad that I would now get to have a hot shower and another break.

Once enough of us had returned to a safe area near the scene, we climbed into the car that was there and tuned the heaters up full-blast. We then spent 20 minutes trying to navigate our way out of the place, continually driving up dead-end roads and streets that took us back the way we had come. Stopping to ask directions was useless, as the staff on the various cordon points had been called in from as far away as Wellington, and had no idea either. We finally made it back and pulled to a grateful halt in the yard at HQ. Again, I tidied up a load of paperwork from the night's shift and caught a ride back to the motel.

Once again I spent half an hour in the shower, scrubbing the face paint off, before collapsing into a grateful but tired heap on the bed. I snuggled down under the covers and put a pillow over my head to drown out any sounds that might filter in. By now I was too tired to play through any of the evening's events in my mind and fell into a deep slumber soon after my head hit the pillow. Unfortunately it didn't last long, and when I woke again I sent out texts to those who I knew were still at the base, asking for updates. No change. He still hadn't been found.

I listlessly turned on the TV, trying to find additional news; then, after two hours, gave up and tried again to sleep. Another hour later and I was woken by a hammering on my door. By the time I stuck my head out, the door-hammerer – it was G – had gone, but I got the news that we were going home. The gunman had been found dead. A post-mortem later showed that he had died of a single, self-inflicted gunshot to his head. It was likely to have occurred on the previous afternoon (the Friday).

What happened in Napier that Thursday was a terrible tragedy. One police officer lost his life, two other officers and one civilian were seriously wounded. The person responsible for all that carnage took his own life, taking away any possibility of asking him why. Afterward, many heros were spoken of, their actions in saving (in some cases) people they didn't even know admirable and incredibly brave. Many people will never get over the events of that day. They are certainly indelibly marked in my mind. While we can all comment on what could have prevented the tragedy, it doesn't change the fact that it happened. I will say one thing, though. From the very small part I played and from what I saw and heard being done, it reinforced why I am so proud to be a member of the New Zealand Police.

26

THE LAST CHAPTER

Policing is a job that has always afforded many opportunities to those who are willing to take them. It's diverse in nature. It's sad, dangerous, exhausting, exhilarating, hilarious, embarrassing, and always unpredictable. The people you have to deal with – both in the community and within the police force – can at times frustrate you beyond reason, and at other times reduce you to tears with their compassion or humility.

Over my time in blue, many officers have lost their lives in the line of duty, and that is a tragedy. While none of us goes out to work each day with a belief that this will actually happen to us, it is an ever-present consideration. Let's face it: you never know which day is going to be your last, something I always reflect on when the news reaches me that a police colleague has been killed or injured in their line of work. Did they have any inkling that this day was not going to be like any other? Do you know? Can you prepare?

Somehow – in the blink of an eye really – I managed to clock up over 17 years of service, and on the day I received my Long Service, Good Conduct medal I felt really proud. I know I use that word a lot, but I can't think of any others that fit. I had no idea I would still be in the job after this long. Looking back over what feels to be, so far, a short policing career, I know I have had a go at every job that interested me. I have been a police negotiator, a personal protection officer, and an AOS member. I have been a front-line police officer, a detective in the CIB, a community police officer, an intelligence officer and a detective sergeant. And there are still more jobs to have a go at; I just haven't decided which ones yet.

One very final note: I have not written this book on behalf of the New Zealand Police. It is not a recruiting or a marketing tool. In fact, I had to jump through the usual hoops to get it published, as I'm a still-serving member of the Police. There is every chance that when it is released, something will have happened in policing to make the public dislike us again and raise suspicion about this book's 'timing'. Our popularity as police, as always, runs in ebbs and flows and neither can be predicted. This book is simply me wanting to share with you something that holds great interest for me, and which I am passionate about. Thanks for taking the time to read it.

Glossary

2-I/C second-in-command

AOS Armed Offenders Squad

ballistic vest an armoured vest that stops bullets penetrating

BET Battle Efficiency Test

camo camouflage

cannabis tinnie a ready-for-sale packet of a small quantity of cannabis wrapped in tinfoil

cherry-picker a crane with a bucket for workers to stand in

CIB Criminal Investigation Branch

Clayton's a non-alcoholic drink made to resemble whisky, available in the 1970s and 1980s. The word is now used to describe a substitute for the real thing

Columbine High School a school in the USA where two senior students, Eric Harris and Dylan Klebold, shot and killed 12 other students and one teacher on 20 April 1999, then committed suicide

comms police communications centre

Cooper's a 12-minute run test

F61 General Instruction on the use of firearms by police; *see also* GIs

FX simulated ammunition ('simmunition')

GIs General Instructions and Guidelines issued by the Commissioner of Police

Glock   a 17-round pistol used by the New Zealand Police; when used by specialist squads, may have a torch attached

IED   improvised explosive device

karaoke   a loud hailer

Kevlar   a non-penetrating armour used for ballistic protection in the AOS, such as body armour and helmets

LAV   light armoured vehicle

M4   .223 long firearm, also known as a Bushmaster

MOE   mode of entry (kit)

NVGs   night-vision goggles

OC   pepper spray

PCT   physical competency test used by the New Zealand Police

PNT   Police Negotiating Team

PT   physical training

rebar   reinforcing bar; a length of metal roughly the same size and weight as a long firearm

RFL   Required Fitness Level – an army term

RV   rendezvous

SAR   Search and Rescue

SAS   Special Air Service

simmunition   *see* FX

SFP   safe forward point

SRBA   stab-resistant body armour

stunnies   stun grenades

TOETs   tests of elementary training skills, related to weaponry

Worzel Gummidge   a scarecrow character from a series of children's books by Barbara Euphan Todd

Zero Alpha   AOS control base during an operation

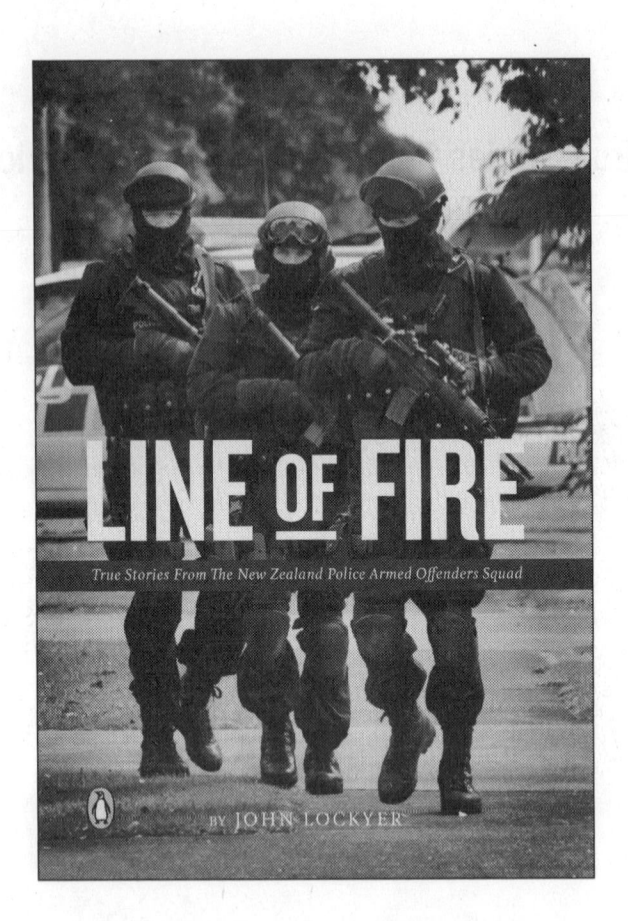

LINE OF FIRE

True Stories From The New Zealand Police Armed Offenders Squad

BY JOHN LOCKYER

LINE OF FIRE

True Stories from the New Zealand Police Armed Offenders Squads

John Lockyer

The New Zealand Police Armed Offenders Squads are never far from the headlines. Called out to the worst-case scenarios in which lives are in danger, their exploits make them a media magnet. But despite this, little is known about the people behind the masks.

In conjunction with the TV documentary series *Line of Fire*, this book seeks to go behind the public façade of the AOS to get inside the heads of men and women who have served in the squads through the five decades of their existence. To find out what sort of person willingly steps into the line of fire to ensure that the country we live in is a safer place.

JOHN LOCKYER

NZ Detectives

True stories
from the New Zealand Police
Criminal Investigation
Branch

NZ DETECTIVES
True stories from the New Zealand Police Criminal Investigation Branch
John Lockyer

The detectives of the New Zealand Police Criminal Investigation Branch (CIB) are charged with investigating and solving serious crime.

To outsmart and defeat New Zealand's hardened organised crime rings, the CIB employ the most sophisticated techniques and technologies available. But at the end of the day, fighting crime demands an unflinching commitment to the case and an old-fashioned nose for the truth.

In conjunction with the television documentary series NZ Detectives, this book goes behind closed doors to meet former and current detectives dedicated to the pursuit of the truth — men and women whose grit and dedication cracked some of the country's biggest criminal cases.